U.S. Department of Justice
Office of Justice Programs
Bureau of Justice Statistics

SPECIAL REPORT

APRIL 2014

NCJ 244205

Recidivism of Prisoners Released in 30 States in 2005: Patterns from 2005 to 2010

Matthew R. Durose, Alexia D. Cooper, Ph.D., and Howard N. Snyder, Ph.D., *BJS Statisticians*

Overall, 67.8% of the 404,638 state prisoners released in 2005 in 30 states were arrested within 3 years of release, and 76.6% were arrested within 5 years of release (figure 1). Among prisoners released in 2005 in 23 states with available data on inmates returned to prison, 49.7% had either a parole or probation violation or an arrest for a new offense within 3 years that led to imprisonment, and 55.1% had a parole or probation violation or an arrest that led to imprisonment within 5 years.

While prior Bureau of Justice Statistics (BJS) prisoner recidivism reports tracked inmates for 3 years following release, this report used a 5-year follow-up period. The longer window provides supplementary information for policymakers and practitioners on the officially recognized criminal behavior of released prisoners. While 20.5% of released prisoners not arrested within 2 years of release were arrested in the third year, the percentage fell to 13.3% among those who had not been arrested within 4 years. The longer recidivism period also provides a more complete assessment of the number and types of crimes committed by released persons in the years following their release.

FIGURE 1

Recidivism of prisoners released in 30 states in 2005, by time from release to first arrest that led to recidivating event

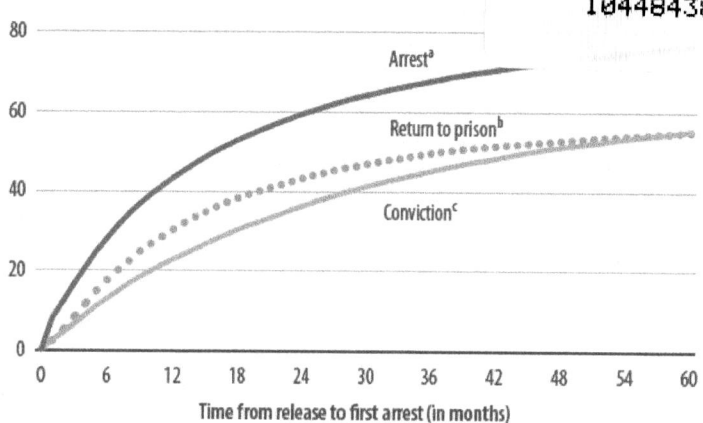

Note: Prisoners were tracked for 5 years following release in 30 states. Some states were excluded from the specific measures of recidivism. See *Methodology*.
[a]Based on time from release to first arrest among inmates released in 30 states.
[b]Based on time from release to first arrest that led to a prison sentence or first prison admission for a technical violation without a new sentence among inmates released in 23 states.
[c]Based on time from release to first arrest that led to a conviction among inmates released in 29 states.
Source: Bureau of Justice Statistics, Recidivism of State Prisoners Released in 2005 data collection.

HIGHLIGHTS

Among state prisoners released in 30 states in 2005—

- About two-thirds (67.8%) of released prisoners were arrested for a new crime within 3 years, and three-quarters (76.6%) were arrested within 5 years.

- Within 5 years of release, 82.1% of property offenders were arrested for a new crime, compared to 76.9% of drug offenders, 73.6% of public order offenders, and 71.3% of violent offenders.

- More than a third (36.8%) of all prisoners who were arrested within 5 years of release were arrested within the first 6 months after release, with more than half (56.7%) arrested by the end of the first year.

- Two in five (42.3%) released prisoners were either not arrested or arrested once in the 5 years after their release.

- A sixth (16.1%) of released prisoners were responsible for almost half (48.4%) of the nearly 1.2 million arrests that occurred in the 5-year follow-up period.

- An estimated 10.9% of released prisoners were arrested in a state other than the one that released them during the 5-year follow-up period.

- Within 5 years of release, 84.1% of inmates who were age 24 or younger at release were arrested, compared to 78.6% of inmates ages 25 to 39 and 69.2% of those age 40 or older.

BJS

Factors contributing to differences with prior BJS studies

Policymakers, practitioners, researchers, and the general public may be interested in understanding how the 2005 prisoner recidivism rates in this report compare with those in the previous BJS recidivism study that measured prisoners released in 1994. While both the 1994 and 2005 studies were based on systematic samples of persons released from state prisons, direct comparisons between the published recidivism statistics should not be made.

Adjustments for some differences in the 1994 and 2005 prison populations are possible

One reason for not directly comparing the 1994 and 2005 recidivism estimates relates to differences in the attributes of the prisoners included in the two samples. The number of states contributing released prisoners to the study increased from 15 in 1994 to 30 in 2005. To control for this difference, BJS conducted analyses that limited the comparison to the post-release arrest rates among the inmates released in the 12 states (California, Florida, Maryland, Michigan, Minnesota, New Jersey, New York, North Carolina, Ohio, Oregon, Texas, and Virginia) that participated in both studies. Among the inmates released in these 12 states, an estimated 66.9% of the 249,657 inmates released in 1994 were arrested for a new crime within 3 years, compared to an estimated 69.3% of the 286,829 inmates released in 2005—a 2.4 percentage point difference.

Another difference between the two studies involved the demographic and offending characteristics of prisoners released from the state prisons, attributes known to be related to recidivism. For example, the proportion of inmates who were age 40 or older at release increased from 17.2% in the 1994 sample to 32.1% in the 2005 sample. In addition, the proportion who were in prison for a violent offense increased from 22.4% in the 1994 sample to 27.4% in the 2005 sample (table 1).

TABLE 1

Characteristics of prisoners released in 12 states in 1994 and 2005

Characteristic	1994	2005
All released prisoners	100%	100%
Sex		
Male	91.2%	89.9%
Female	8.8	10.1
Race/Hispanic origin		
White[a]	32.2%	35.4%
Black/African American[a]	46.2	40.5
Hispanic/Latino	20.9	22.4
Other[a,b]	0.7	1.8
Age at release		
24 or younger	20.6%	16.9%
25–29	22.7	18.9
30–34	23.0	16.0
35–39	16.6	16.1
40 or older	17.2	32.1
Most serious commitment offense		
Violent	22.4%	27.4%
Property	33.2	29.1
Drug	33.0	31.4
Public order[c]	11.4	12.1
Number of released prisoners	249,657	286,829

Note: Estimates based on a sample of 29,387 prisoners released in 1994 and a sample of 34,649 prisoners released in 2005 in the 12 states that participated in both studies (California, Florida, Maryland, Michigan, Minnesota, New Jersey, New York, North Carolina, Ohio, Oregon, Texas, and Virginia). Data on the sex of prisoners released in 1994 were known for 100% of cases, race and Hispanic origin for 99.9%, and age at release for nearly 100%. Data on the sex of prisoners released in 2005 were known for 100% of cases, race and Hispanic origin for 99.8%, and age at release for 100%. See appendix table 1 for standard errors.

[a]Excludes persons of Hispanic or Latino origin.

[b]Includes persons identified as American Indian or Alaska Native; Asian, Native Hawaiian, or other Pacific Islander; and persons of other races.

[c]Includes cases in which the prisoner's most serious offense was unspecified.

Source: Bureau of Justice Statistics, Recidivism of State Prisoners Released in 1994 and 2005 data collections.

Continued on next page.

Factors contributing to differences with prior BJS studies (continued)

BJS standardized the demographic (i.e., sex, race, Hispanic origin, and age) and commitment offense distribution of the 2005 cohort to the distribution of the 1994 cohort to control for the effects these factors had on the overall recidivism estimates. (See *Methodology* for more information.) These calculations produced the 3-year arrest rate of prisoners released in 2005 that would have been observed if the 2005 release cohort had the characteristics of the 1994 cohort. After adjusting for these compositional differences, the estimated percentage of the 2005 released prisoners who were arrested within 3 years rose to 71.6%, a recidivism rate 4.7% greater than the 1994 estimate (66.9%) (table 2). However, these analyses only partially address the differences between the 1994 and 2005 studies.

Additional death records on released prisoners leads to increases in recidivism rates

A critical difference between the 1994 and 2005 studies was the use of the Social Security Administration's public Death Master File (DMF) in the 2005 study to identify individuals who died during the follow-up period. (See *Methodology* for more information.) These individuals should be removed from the analysis because they artificially reduce the calculated recidivism rates. The 1994 study limited the identification of released prisoners who died to those who had an indication of death on their criminal history record (i.e., rap sheet). The 2005 study supplemented the death information obtained from the FBI's Interstate Identification Index (III) with the DMF data. Based on both sources of information, 1,595 of the 70,878 inmates sampled for the 2005 study had died during the 5-year follow-up period. Less than 10% of those deaths were captured in the fingerprint verified death information that criminal justice agencies submitted to the FBI's III system. If the DMF data had not been used in the 2005 study and the rap sheets of these individuals had been included in the analyses, the estimated 5-year recidivism rate would have been about one-half of one percent lower.

Effects of the criminal history record improvements on recidivism research are difficult to quantify

Direct comparisons between the published recidivism rates from the 1994 and the new 2005 study are also difficult due to the completeness of the criminal history records available to BJS at the time of the data collections. Both studies were based on fingerprint-verified automated rap sheets stored in the FBI and the state repositories. While both studies relied on records within the FBI's III system for information on the arrests and prosecutions that occurred outside of the states that released the inmates, the 2005 study used new data collection capabilities to directly access the criminal history record systems of all 50 states and obtain more comprehensive out-of-state information than what was available for the 1994 study. (See *Methodology* for more information.) In addition, BJS was unable to obtain any out-of-state criminal history information on the prisoners released in one state in the 1994 study due to a nondisclosure agreement.

Continued on next page.

TABLE 2
Population-adjusted percent of prisoners arrested for a new crime within 3 years following release in 12 states in 1994 and 2005, by demographic characteristics and most serious commitment offense

Characteristic	1994	2005[a]
All released prisoners	66.9%	71.6%**
Sex		
Male	67.8%	72.5%**
Female	57.2	62.9**
Race/Hispanic origin		
White[b]	61.7%	68.8%**
Black/African American[b]	71.9	74.0**
Hispanic/Latino	64.6	70.7**
Other[b,c]	53.6	72.6**
Age at release		
24 or younger	74.7%	78.2%**
25–29	69.8	73.4**
30–34	68.3	70.3
35–39	66.3	71.8**
40 or older	52.4	62.9**
Most serious commitment offense		
Violent	60.9%	65.6%**
Property	73.2	77.6**
Drug	66.3	71.4**
Public order[d]	62.2	66.9**
Number of released prisoners	249,658	286,011

Note: Estimates based on a sample of 29,387 prisoners released in 1994 and a sample of 34,649 prisoners released in 2005 in the 12 states that participated in both studies. See appendix table 2 for standard errors.

**Difference between the estimate on the 1994 cohort and the estimate on the standardized 2005 cohort was statistically significant at or above the 95% confidence interval.

[a]Estimates of inmates released in 2005 have been standardized to the distribution of inmates released in 1994 by sex, race, Hispanic origin, age at release, and most serious commitment offense. The unadjusted estimate for the 2005 cohort was 69.3%.

[b]Excludes persons of Hispanic or Latino origin.

[c]Includes persons identified as American Indian or Alaska Native; Asian, Native Hawaiian, or other Pacific Islander; and persons of other races.

[d]Includes cases in which the prisoner's most serious offense was unspecified.

Source: Bureau of Justice Statistics, Recidivism of State Prisoners Released in 1994 and 2005 data collections.

Factors contributing to differences with prior BJS studies (continued)

The improved reporting of arrests and prosecutions maintained by the FBI and state repositories in the decade between the two studies also resulted in more complete documentation of the official criminal records of prisoners released in 2005. The quality of rap sheets has improved since the mid-1990s due to efforts funded by individual states and by BJS's National Criminal History Improvement Program (NCHIP), which awarded more than $500 million over this period to states for criminal history record improvements. As a result, many existing paper arrest records were automated and stored within a computerized criminal history system. Also, the growth in the use of automated fingerprint technology (e.g., livescan) reduced the proportion of illegible fingerprint images delivered to the repositories, resulting in more arrests and court adjudications being recorded on the rap sheets.

In addition, while local law enforcement agencies historically limited their criminal history repository submissions to arrests for felonies and serious misdemeanors, the reporting of less serious misdemeanors or minor infractions expanded during this time, although it is unknown whether this increase is due to changes in reporting practices or changes in the criminal behaviors of the released prisoners. In general, violent crimes are considered to be more serious than public order offenses. Among the prisoners who were arrested for a new crime within 3 years, public order offenses made up 36.0% of the first post-release arrests for the 2005 cohort, compared to 22.9% of the first post-release arrests for the 1994 cohort (table 3). Violent offenses accounted for 14.8% of the first post-release arrests for the 2005 cohort, compared to 18.8% of the first post-release arrests for the 1994 cohort.*

---

*These estimates were based on prisoners released in the 11 states in both studies that included charge descriptions in their criminal history records.

TABLE 3
First arrest charge of prisoners arrested for a new crime within 3 years following release in 11 states in 1994 and 2005

Most serious arrest charge	1994	2005
All released prisoners	100%	100%
Violent	18.8%	14.8%
Property	28.8	23.6
Drug	29.5	25.6
Public order*	22.9	36.0
Estimated number of prisoners with a post-release arrest	161,000	191,000

Note: Estimates based on a sample of 27,788 prisoners released in 1994 and a sample of 32,155 prisoners released in 2005 in the 11 states that participated in both studies and included charge descriptions in their arrest records. Number of arrests was rounded to the nearest 1,000. First arrest may include multiple charges; the most serious charge is reported in this table. See appendix table 3 for standard errors.

*Includes cases in which the prisoner's most serious offense was unspecified.

Source: Bureau of Justice Statistics, Recidivism of State Prisoners Released in 1994 and 2005 data collections.

Continued on next page.

Factors contributing to differences with prior BJS studies (continued)

As a result of the improvements to the nation's criminal history records, the rap sheets of prisoners released in 2005 likely captured more complete offending histories than the rap sheets used in the 1994 study. These improvements would have resulted in higher observed recidivism rates in 2005 than in 1994, even if the two samples had the same true recidivism rates.

BJS conducted a test of this assumption by comparing the recidivism rates of the 1994 and 2005 samples using only new arrests for a violent offense. The logic behind this test was that, while the rap sheets for the 2005 cohort may contain more arrests overall and more arrests for minor offenses, arrests for violent offenses should be well represented in both sets of rap sheets. Using this more serious indictor of criminal behavior and controlling for cohort differences in offender demographics and most serious commitment offense, the percentage of released prisoners who were arrested for a violent crime within 3 years following release did not differ significantly between the 1994 (21.3%) and 2005 (21.8%) cohorts (table 4).

The stability in the 1994 and 2005 recidivism rates when recidivism is measured as a new arrest for a violent crime and the difference observed when recidivism is measured as a new offense for any offense raises questions about the overall consistency of rap sheet content between the 1994 and 2005 studies. More research is required to better understand the effects of rap sheet improvements on observed recidivism rates. However, given the limited empirical data currently available on the state-level changes in rap sheet content since the mid-1990s, the effects of rap sheet improvements on the observed recidivism rates cannot be quantified, and statistical adjustments for their effects cannot be made. Therefore, it is not advisable to compare the 2005 recidivism rates in this report with those found in earlier BJS reports until we have a deeper understanding of the changes in rap sheet content.

TABLE 4
Population-adjusted percent of prisoners arrested for a violent crime within 3 years following release in 11 states in 1994 and 2005, by demographic characteristics and most serious commitment offense

Characteristic	1994	2005[a]
All released prisoners	21.3%	21.8%
Sex		
Male	22.4%	22.7%
Female	10.2	13.1**
Race/Hispanic origin		
White[b]	16.4%	19.3%**
Black/African American[b]	26.2	25.3
Hispanic/Latino	18.7	18.5
Other[b,c]	19.0	18.5
Age at release		
24 or younger	28.9%	28.6%
25–29	23.9	24.8
30–34	21.2	20.1
35–39	17.3	19.5
40 or older	12.7	14.3
Most serious commitment offense		
Violent	27.0%	24.8%**
Property	21.4	22.2
Drug	18.4	19.5
Public order[d]	17.9	21.4**
Number of released prisoners	241,448	276,218

Note: Estimates based on a sample of 27,788 prisoners released in 1994 and a sample of 32,155 prisoners released in 2005 in the 11 states that participated in both studies and included charge descriptions in their arrest records. See appendix table 4 for standard errors.

**Difference between the estimate on the 1994 cohort and the estimate on the standardized 2005 cohort was statistically significant at or above the 95% confidence interval.

[a]Estimates of inmates released in 2005 have been standardized to the distribution of inmates released in 1994 by sex, race, Hispanic origin, age at release, and most serious commitment offense. The unadjusted estimate for the 2005 cohort was 20.1%.

[b]Excludes persons of Hispanic or Latino origin.

[c]Includes persons identified as American Indian or Alaska Native; Asian, Native Hawaiian, or other Pacific Islander; and persons of other races.

[d]Includes cases in which the prisoner's most serious offense was unspecified.

Source: Bureau of Justice Statistics, Recidivism of State Prisoners Released in 1994 and 2005 data collections.

Criminal history and prison records were used to document recidivism patterns

This study estimates the recidivism patterns of 404,638 persons released in 2005 from state prisons in 30 states. In 2005, these states held 76% of the U.S. population and were responsible for 77% of the prisoners released from U.S. prisons (not shown). A representative sample of inmates released in 2005 was developed for each of the 30 states using data reported by state departments of corrections to BJS's National Corrections Reporting Program (NCRP), yielding a final sample of 68,597 persons. (For a complete description of the sampling and weighting procedures, see *Methodology*.) Using information contained in state and federal criminal history records (i.e., rap sheets) and the records of state departments of corrections, this report details the arrest, adjudication, conviction, and incarceration experiences of these former inmates within and outside of the state that released them for a 5-year period following their release from prison.

This research has attempted to minimize the effect on recidivism statistics posed by state variations in criminal history reporting policies, coding practices, and coverage. The analysis excluded arrest events in the rap sheets that were not commonly recorded by all states (e.g., arrests for many types of traffic offenses). The analysis also excluded sections of the rap sheets that recorded the issuance of a warrant as an arrest event when no arrest actually occurred. Some variations in the content of rap sheets remained and cannot be remediated, such as the nature of the charging decision. For example, when an inmate on parole is arrested for committing a burglary, some local law enforcement agencies coded the arrest offense as a parole violation, some coded it as a burglary, and others coded both the burglary and the parole violation. Given that this is often a local coding decision, it is difficult to discern from the contents of the rap sheets which charging approach was employed at each arrest.

Along with these coding variations, it is commonly assumed that the information derived from criminal history repositories understates the criminal histories of offenders, especially information on actions that occurred over 20 years ago. While it cannot be quantified at this time, the common perception is that, through targeted funding and the efforts of criminal justice practitioners across the country, the quality and completeness of rap sheets has improved so that they provide better assessments of recidivism patterns.

Among the 404,638 prisoners released in 30 states in 2005, 31.8% were in prison for a drug offense, 29.8% for a property offense, 25.7% for a violent offense, and 12.7% for a public order offense (table 5). Nearly 9 in 10 (89.3%) of released prisoners were male. More than a third (36.9%) of these persons were under age 30 at release, and about a third (31.5%) were age 40 or older. The proportions of non-Hispanic black (40.1%) and non-Hispanic white (39.9%) prisoners were similar. An estimated 25.7% of the released prisoners had 4 or fewer prior arrests, while 43.2% had 10 or more. Half of the released prisoners had 3 or more prior convictions.

TABLE 5
Characteristics of prisoners released in 30 states in 2005

Characteristic	Percent
All released prisoners	100%
Sex	
Male	89.3%
Female	10.7
Race/Hispanic origin	
White[a]	39.9%
Black/African American[a]	40.1
Hispanic/Latino	17.7
Other[a,b]	2.4
Age at release	
24 or younger	17.6%
25–29	19.3
30–34	15.9
35–39	15.7
40 or older	31.5
Most serious commitment offense	
Violent	25.7%
Property	29.8
Drug	31.8
Public order[c]	12.7
Number of prior arrests per released prisoner[d]	
2 or fewer	11.5%
3–4	14.2
5–9	31.1
10 or more	43.2
Mean number	10.6
Median number	7.8
Number of prior convictions per released prisoner[d]	
Mean number	4.9
Median number	3.1
Number of released prisoners	404,638

Note: Data on the prisoner's sex were known for 100% of cases, race and Hispanic origin for nearly 100%, and age at release for 100%. See appendix table 5 for standard errors.

[a]Excludes persons of Hispanic or Latino origin.

[b]Includes persons identified as American Indian or Alaska Native; Asian, Native Hawaiian, or other Pacific Islander; and persons of other races.

[c]Includes 0.8% of cases in which the prisoner's most serious offense was unspecified.

[d]Includes arrest and conviction that resulted in the imprisonment.

Source: Bureau of Justice Statistics, Recidivism of State Prisoners Released in 2005 data collection.

1 in 10 state prisoners had an out-of-state arrest within 5 years of release

An estimated 24.7% of the released prisoners had a prior arrest in a state other than the one that released them (table 6). About 1 in 10 (10.9%) released prisoners were arrested at least once outside the state that released them during the 5-year follow-up period. These statistics show the limitations of recidivism studies that only have access to in-state criminal history information.

3 in 4 state prisoners were arrested within 5 years of release

Within 1 year after their release from state prison, 43.4% of prisoners had been arrested either in or outside of the state that released them. This percentage grew each year, increasing to 59.5% by the end of the second year, 67.8% by the end of the third year, and 76.6% by the end of the 5-year follow-up period.

Another way to view these recidivism statistics is to consider how quickly those who recidivated actually did so. More than a third (36.8%) of all released prisoners who were arrested within 5 years of release were arrested within the first 6 months, with more than half (56.7%) arrested by the end of the first year (not shown).

The longer released prisoners went without being arrested, the less likely they were to be arrested within the 5-year period. For example, compared to the arrest rate of 43.4% in the first year after release, 28.5% of persons not arrested in the first year were arrested for the first time in the second year following their release from prison (figure 2). Similarly, for those not arrested by the end of the second year, 20.5% were arrested by the end of the third year, with the arrest rate falling to 16.1% in the fourth year. Finally, 13.3% of released prisoners who went 4 years without an arrest were arrested in the fifth year.

The 404,638 persons released in 2005 were arrested an estimated 1,173,000 times in the 5 years after release (table 7). While some of them had a large number of arrests in the follow-up period (maximum of 81), most did not. Among all released prisoners, the average number of arrests in the 5-year period was 2.9, while the median number of arrests was 1.5. About 2 in 5 (42.3%) of all releasees were arrested no more than once in the 5-year period, and more than half (57.6%) had fewer than 3 arrests in the 5 years following their release. Despite this, among released prisoners who were arrested at least once

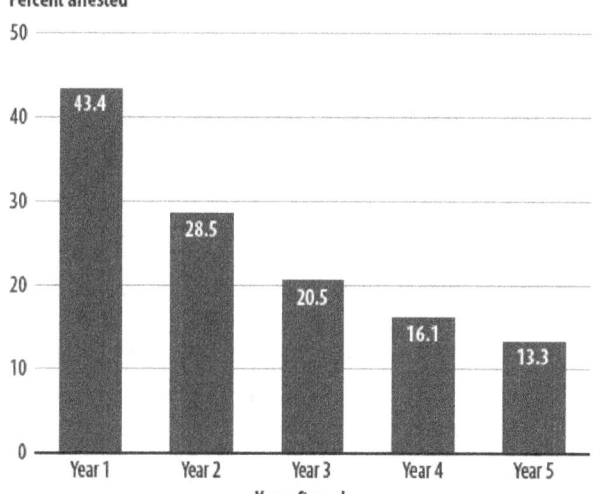

FIGURE 2
Percent of prisoners arrested during the year who had not been arrested since release in 30 states in 2005

Percent arrested

Year after release	Percent
Year 1	43.4
Year 2	28.5
Year 3	20.5
Year 4	16.1
Year 5	13.3

Note: The denominators for the annual rates were 404,638 for year 1; 229,035 for year 2; 163,679 for year 3; 130,128 for year 4; and 109,186 for year 5. The numerators include persons arrested in the year who had not been arrested since release. See appendix table 7 for standard errors.
Source: Bureau of Justice Statistics, Recidivism of State Prisoners Released in 2005 data collection.

TABLE 6
Out-of-state arrests of prisoners released in 30 states in 2005

Out-of-state arrests	Percent
Prior to release	
1 or more	24.7%
1–4	17.5
5–9	4.3
10 or more	2.9
Post-release	
1 or more	10.9%
1–4	9.6
5–9	1.1
10 or more	0.2

Note: Prisoners were tracked for 5 years following release. Arrested out-of-state includes arrests that occurred in states other than the one that released the prisoner in 2005. See appendix table 6 for standard errors.
Source: Bureau of Justice Statistics, Recidivism of State Prisoners Released in 2005 data collection.

TABLE 7
Post-release arrests of prisoners released in 30 states in 2005

Post-release arrests	Percent
All released prisoners	100%
None	23.4
1	18.9
2	15.3
3	11.5
4	8.5
5	6.4
6 or more	16.1
Estimated number of post-release arrests	1,173,000
Mean number per released prisoner	2.9
Median number per released prisoner	1.5
Number of released prisoners	404,638

Note: Prisoners were tracked for 5 years following release. Number of post-release arrests was rounded to the nearest 1,000. See appendix table 8 for standard errors.
Source: Bureau of Justice Statistics, Recidivism of State Prisoners Released in 2005 data collection. Source: Bureau of Justice Statistics, Recidivism of State Prisoners Released in 2005 data collection.

during the 5-year follow-up period, three-quarters (75.4%) were arrested again during the 5-year period (not shown). About a sixth (16.1%) of released prisoners were responsible for about half (48.4%) of the 1,173,000 arrests of released prisoners that occurred in the 5-year follow-up period.

Prisoners released after serving time for a property offense were the most likely to be arrested

Within 5 years of release, 82.1% of prisoners who had been committed for a property offense had been arrested for a new offense, followed by 76.9% of those committed for a drug offense (figure 3 and table 8). Offenders sentenced for a violent (71.3%) or public order offense (73.6%) were the least likely to be arrested after release.

This general pattern of recidivism was maintained across the 5-year follow-up period. A year after release from prison, the recidivism rate of prisoners sentenced for a property offense (50.3 %) was higher than the rates for drug (42.3%), public order (40.1%), and violent (38.4%) offenders. Among violent offenders, the annual recidivism rates of prisoners sentenced for homicide or sexual assault were lower than those sentenced for assault or robbery across the 5-year period. Among property offenders, inmates committed for larceny or motor vehicle theft had higher annual recidivism rates than those committed for fraud or forgery across the 5-year period.

FIGURE 3

Recidivism of prisoners released in 30 states in 2005, by most serious commitment offense and time from release to first arrest

Percent arrested

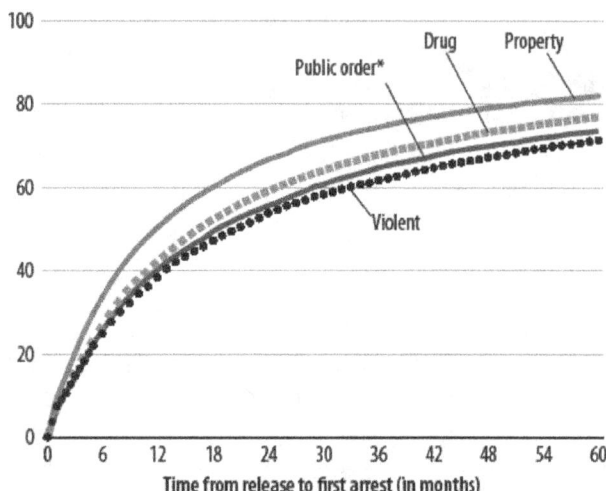

Note: Prisoners were tracked for 5 years following release.
*Includes 0.8% of cases in which the prisoner's most serious offense was unspecified.
Source: Bureau of Justice Statistics, Recidivism of State Prisoners Released in 2005 data collection.

TABLE 8

Recidivism of prisoners released in 30 states in 2005, by most serious commitment offense and time from release to first arrest

Most serious commitment offense	Cumulative percent of released prisoners arrested within—					
	6 months	1 year	2 years	3 years	4 years	5 years
All released prisoners	28.2%	43.4%	59.5%	67.8%	73.0%	76.6%
Violent	24.9%	38.4%	53.8%	61.6%	67.2%	71.3%
Homicide[a]	12.5	21.5	33.9	41.5	47.0	51.2
Murder	10.1	18.8	30.4	37.8	43.6	47.9
Nonnegligent manslaughter	17.3	27.7	39.4	46.0	51.5	55.7
Negligent manslaughter	13.2	21.9	35.5	43.7	48.8	53.0
Rape/sexual assault	20.8	30.9	43.7	50.9	56.0	60.1
Robbery	25.8	41.0	58.6	66.9	72.8	77.0
Assault	27.9	42.6	58.9	67.1	72.9	77.1
Other	28.7	43.4	56.6	63.0	66.9	70.4
Property	33.6%	50.3%	66.7%	74.5%	79.1%	82.1%
Burglary	31.0	48.7	65.8	73.9	78.9	81.8
Larceny/motor vehicle theft	39.3	56.2	70.8	77.6	81.6	84.1
Fraud/forgery	27.7	42.2	60.0	68.6	73.2	77.0
Other	33.2	49.5	66.6	75.5	80.9	83.6
Drug	26.9%	42.3%	59.1%	67.9%	73.3%	76.9%
Possession	28.7	44.5	60.7	69.6	75.2	78.3
Trafficking	26.9	41.5	58.0	66.6	71.9	75.4
Other	25.3	41.4	59.3	68.3	73.6	78.1
Public order	25.6%	40.1%	55.6%	64.7%	69.9%	73.6%
Weapons	35.3	49.1	65.1	73.1	76.9	79.5
Driving under the influence	11.9	22.1	37.2	48.0	54.9	59.9
Other[b]	27.8	44.9	60.4	69.2	74.1	77.9

Note: Prisoners were tracked for 5 years following release. Inmates could have been in prison for more than one offense; the most serious one is reported in this table. See appendix table 9 for standard errors.
[a]Includes cases in which the type of homicide was unspecified, not shown separately.
[b]Includes 0.8% of cases in which the prisoner's most serious offense was unspecified.
Source: Bureau of Justice Statistics, Recidivism of State Prisoners Released in 2005 data collection.

Within the first 5 years of release from state prison in 2005, an estimated 28.6% of inmates were arrested for a violent offense (table 9). Among all released inmates, an estimated 1.7% were arrested for rape or sexual assault, and 23.0% were arrested for assault. During the 5-year follow-up period, the majority (58.0%) of released prisoners were arrested for a public order offense. About 1 in 4 (25.3%) released prisoners were arrested for a probation or parole violation. An estimated 39.9% were arrested for some other public order offense, including failure to appear and obstruction of justice, which in some jurisdictions may be the legal response to probation or parole violations. Other public order offenses include drunkenness, disorderly conduct, liquor law violation, or a family-related offense.

Compared to inmates incarcerated for a property (28.5%), drug (24.8%), or public order offense (29.2%), a higher percentage of inmates incarcerated for a violent offense were arrested for another violent crime (33.1%) during the 5-year period (table 10). A higher percentage of released property offenders were arrested for a property crime (54.0%) than violent, drug, or public order offenders. A higher percentage of released drug offenders were arrested for a drug crime (51.2%) than violent, property, or public order offenders. While these statistics suggest that there was some specialization in the offending behaviors of released inmates, the recidivism patterns also show that released inmates were involved in a wide range of law-violating behaviors.

During the 5-year period, inmates released for a drug offense were less likely than property and public order inmates to be arrested during the 5-year period for a violent offense. In addition, inmates released for a property offense were more likely than violent and public order inmates to be arrested for a drug offense at some point during the 5-year period.

TABLE 9
Recidivism of prisoners released in 30 states in 2005, by type of post-release arrest charge

Post-release arrest charge	Percent of released prisoners arrested within 5 years of release
Any offense	76.6%
Violent	28.6%
Homicide	0.9
Rape/sexual assault	1.7
Robbery	5.5
Assault	23.0
Other	4.0
Property	38.4%
Burglary	10.1
Larceny/motor vehicle theft	21.3
Fraud/forgery	11.9
Other	19.2
Drug	38.8%
Possession	26.8
Trafficking	13.1
Other	19.9
Public order	58.0%
Weapons	9.1
Driving under the influence	9.3
Probation/parole violation	25.3
Other*	39.9

Note: Prisoners were tracked for 5 years following release. Detail may not sum to total because a person may be arrested more than once and each arrest may involve more than one charge. When information on the arrest charge was missing in the criminal history records, the court disposition data were used to describe the charge. See appendix table 10 for standard errors.

*Includes 0.8% of cases in which the prisoner's most serious offense was unspecified.

Source: Bureau of Justice Statistics, Recidivism of State Prisoners Released in 2005 data collection.

TABLE 10
Recidivism of prisoners released in 30 states in 2005, by type of post-release arrest charge and most serious commitment offense

Most serious commitment offense	Percent of released prisoners arrested within 5 years for—				
	Any offense	Violent offense	Property offense	Drug offense	Public order offense*
All released prisoners	76.6%	28.6%	38.4%	38.8%	58.0%
Violent	71.3	33.1	29.7	28.2	55.3
Property	82.1	28.5	54.0	38.5	61.9
Drug	76.9	24.8	33.1	51.2	56.1
Public order*	73.6	29.2	32.7	30.0	59.6

Note: Prisoners were tracked for 5 years following release. Inmates could have been in prison for more than one offense; the most serious one is reported in this table. The numerator for each percent is the number of persons arrested for a charge during the 5-year follow-up period, and the denominator is the number released for each type of commitment offense. Detail may not sum to total because a person may be arrested more than once and each arrest may involve more than one charge. When information on the arrest charge was missing in the criminal history records, the court disposition data were used to describe the charge. See appendix table 11 for standard errors.

*Includes 0.8% of cases in which the prisoner's most serious offense was unspecified.

Source: Bureau of Justice Statistics, Recidivism of State Prisoners Released in 2005 data collection.

Inmate recidivism increased with criminal history

In this study, an inmate's prior criminal history was measured by the number of arrests found on their criminal history records prior to their date of release. A year after release from prison, about a quarter (26.4%) of released inmates with 4 or fewer arrests in their prior criminal record had been arrested, compared to over half (56.1%) of released inmates who had 10 or more prior arrests (figure 4 and table 11).

While recidivism rates increased through the fifth year for both released inmates with 4 or fewer prior arrests and those with 10 or more prior arrests, both groups consistently differed about 30% by the end of the first year. This general pattern remained through the next 4 years. For example, 60.8% of released inmates with 4 or fewer arrests in their prior criminal history had been arrested by the end of the fifth year, compared to 86.5% of released inmates who had 10 or more prior arrests. This finding suggests that the effect of criminal history on recidivism is observable within a year after release and continues into the future.

The negative effect of criminal history on recidivism held across the inmate's most serious incarceration offense category. Inmates incarcerated for a violent offense who had 4 or fewer arrests in their prior criminal history were less likely to be arrested within 5 years (56.3%) than those with 10 or more prior arrests (85.6%) (table 11). This disparity

was also observed among violent offenders arrested within a year of release from prison, as 23.8% of inmates incarcerated for a violent offense were arrested within a year of release, compared to 55.4% of those with 10 or more prior arrests.

FIGURE 4
Recidivism of prisoners released in 30 states in 2005, by prior arrest history and time from release to first arrest

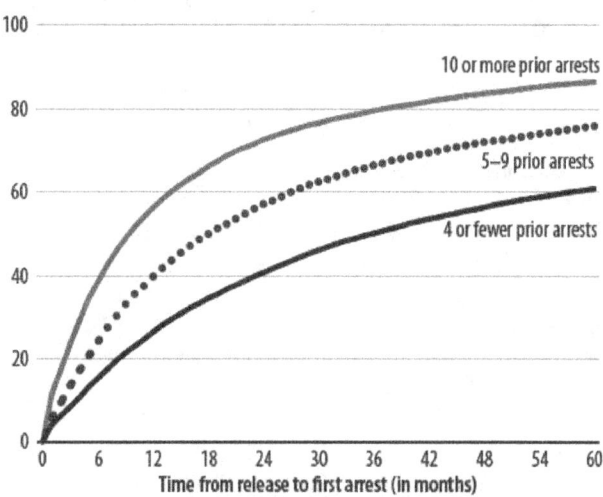

Note: Prisoners were tracked for 5 years following release. Prior arrest history includes the number of times the prisoner was arrested prior to his or her date of release.
Source: Bureau of Justice Statistics, Recidivism of State Prisoners Released in 2005 data collection.

TABLE 11
Recidivism of prisoners released in 30 states in 2005, by prior arrest history, most serious commitment offense, and time from release to first arrest

Prior arrest history and most serious commitment offense	Cumulative percent of released prisoners arrested within—					
	6 months	1 year	2 years	3 years	4 years	5 years
All released prisoners	28.2%	43.4%	59.5%	67.8%	73.0%	76.6%
4 or fewer	15.5%	26.4%	40.7%	50.0%	56.3%	60.8%
Violent	14.2	23.8	36.5	45.3	51.7	56.3
Property	18.3	31.4	47.2	57.4	63.8	67.9
Drug	14.8	25.1	40.8	50.1	56.4	61.2
Public order*	15.9	28.2	41.4	50.8	56.2	60.2
5–9	24.3%	39.8%	57.1%	66.3%	72.0%	75.9%
Violent	23.9	38.0	55.8	64.8	70.4	74.2
Property	28.5	46.2	63.1	71.8	76.9	80.5
Drug	21.6	37.0	55.7	65.5	71.6	75.5
Public order*	22.6	36.5	50.5	59.9	65.9	70.5
10 or more	38.6%	56.1%	72.5%	79.5%	83.7%	86.5%
Violent	38.1	55.4	71.7	77.3	81.7	85.6
Property	42.3	59.9	76.2	82.5	86.2	88.3
Drug	37.0	55.0	71.1	78.8	83.3	86.2
Public order*	33.4	49.5	67.6	76.2	80.6	83.5

Note: Prisoners were tracked for 5 years following release. Inmates could have been in prison for more than one offense; the most serious one is reported in this table. Prior arrest history includes the number of times the prisoner was arrested prior to his or her date of release. See appendix table 12 for standard errors.
*Includes 0.8% of cases in which the prisoner's most serious offense was unspecified.
Source: Bureau of Justice Statistics, Recidivism of State Prisoners Released in 2005 data collection.

Male inmates were arrested at higher rates than female inmates following release

Within 3 years of release from prison, 69.0% of male and 58.5% of female inmates had been arrested at least once (figure 5 and table 12). Five years after release from prison, more than three-quarters (77.6%) of males and two-thirds (68.1%) of females had been arrested. At the end of the first year, the male recidivism rate (44.5%) was about 10 percentage points higher than the female rate (34.4%), a difference that remained relatively stable over the following 4 years.

Among all released prisoners, the average number of arrests in the 5-year period was 2.9 for males and 2.5 for females, while the median number of arrests was 1.6 for males and 1.0 for females (table 13). Half (50.6%) of released females and about 41.3% of released males were arrested no more than once in the 5-year period, while 64.2% of females and 56.8% of males had 2 or fewer arrests over the same period.

The recidivism rates (as measured by arrests) for males were higher than those for females, regardless of the incarceration offense or the recidivism period. At the end of the 5-year follow-up period, the post-release arrest rate for both males and females was highest among those incarcerated for a property offense.

FIGURE 5

Recidivism of prisoners released in 30 states in 2005, by sex of releasee and time from release to first arrest

Percent arrested

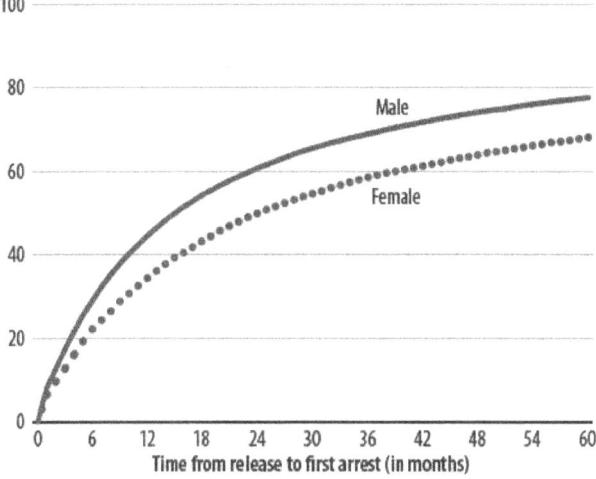

Note: Prisoners were tracked for 5 years following release. Data on prisoner's sex were known for 100% of cases.

Source: Bureau of Justice Statistics, Recidivism of State Prisoners Released in 2005 data collection.

TABLE 13

Post-release arrests of prisoners released in 30 states in 2005, by sex of releasee

Post-release arrests	Male	Female
All released prisoners	100%	100%
None	22.4	31.9
1	18.9	18.7
2	15.5	13.6
3	11.7	9.5
4	8.7	6.9
5	6.4	5.8
6 or more	16.4	13.5
Estimated number of post-release arrests	1,065,000	108,000
Mean number	2.9	2.5
Median number	1.6	1.0
Number of released prisoners	361,469	43,170

Note: Prisoners were tracked for 5 years following release. Number of post-release arrests was rounded to the nearest 1,000. Data on prisoner's sex were known for 100% of cases. See appendix table 14 for standard errors.

Source: Bureau of Justice Statistics, Recidivism of State Prisoners Released in 2005 data collection.

TABLE 12

Recidivism of prisoners released in 30 states in 2005, by sex of releasee, most serious commitment offense, and time from release to first arrest

Sex of releasee and most serious commitment offense	Cumulative percent of released prisoners arrested within—					
	6 months	1 year	2 years	3 years	4 years	5 years
All released prisoners	28.2%	43.4%	59.5%	67.8%	73.0%	76.6%
Male	28.9%	44.5%	60.7%	69.0%	74.1%	77.6%
Violent	25.2	38.9	54.4	62.3	67.9	72.0
Property	35.1	52.3	68.6	76.4	80.9	83.6
Drug	27.6	43.6	60.7	69.4	74.8	78.4
Public order*	26.1	40.8	56.3	65.4	70.5	74.2
Female	22.1%	34.4%	49.8%	58.5%	63.9%	68.1%
Violent	19.8	30.6	44.2	51.9	56.9	60.8
Property	23.8	37.6	54.3	62.6	68.0	72.1
Drug	21.9	33.3	48.1	57.6	62.9	67.3
Public order*	19.2	31.0	47.6	56.1	62.2	66.5

Note: Prisoners were tracked for 5 years following release. Inmates could have been in prison for more than one offense; the most serious one is reported in this table. Data on prisoner's sex were known for 100% of cases. See appendix table 13 for standard errors.

*Includes 0.8% of cases in which the prisoner's most serious offense was unspecified.

Source: Bureau of Justice Statistics, Recidivism of State Prisoners Released in 2005 data collection.

Younger released inmates were arrested at higher rates than older inmates following release

Three years after release, 75.9% of inmates who were age 24 or younger at the time of their release had been arrested for a new offense, compared to 69.7% of those ages 25 to 39 and 60.3% of those age 40 or older (figure 6 and table 14). These patterns were still evident by the end of the fifth year. At the end of the 5-year recidivism period, 84.1% of inmates released at age 24 or younger had been arrested for a new offense, compared to 78.6% of those ages 25 to 39 and 69.2% of those age 40 or older.

FIGURE 6

Recidivism of prisoners released in 30 states in 2005, by age at release and time from release to first arrest

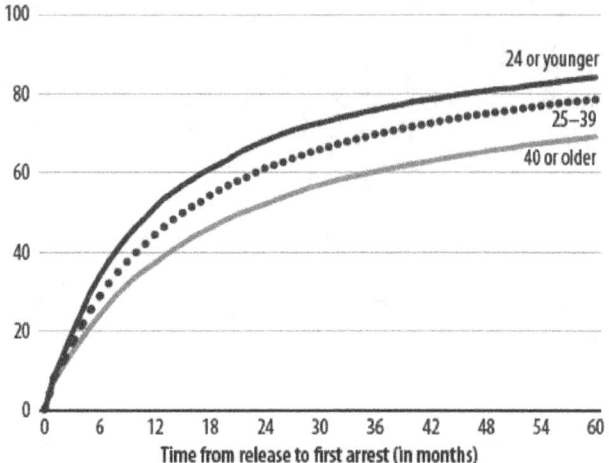

Percent arrested

Time from release to first arrest (in months)

Note: Prisoners were tracked for 5 years following release. Data on prisoner's age were known for 100% of cases.

Source: Bureau of Justice Statistics, Recidivism of State Prisoners Released in 2005 data collection.

TABLE 14

Recidivism of prisoners released in 30 states in 2005, by age at release, most serious commitment offense, and time from release to first arrest

Age at release and most serious commitment offense	Cumulative percent of released prisoners arrested within—					
	6 months	1 year	2 years	3 years	4 years	5 years
All released prisoners	28.2%	43.4%	59.5%	67.8%	73.0%	76.6%
24 or younger	34.0%	51.3%	68.1%	75.9%	80.7%	84.1%
Violent	30.6	45.6	62.7	71.1	76.2	80.4
Property	37.3	55.1	70.9	78.3	82.9	85.8
Drug	31.6	50.0	69.3	77.4	82.4	85.4
Public order*	38.2	56.2	69.8	76.2	80.8	84.7
25–29	29.0%	45.4%	62.1%	71.1%	76.6%	80.3%
Violent	25.1	39.6	56.5	66.4	72.7	76.7
Property	34.2	51.1	67.3	75.4	80.0	83.5
Drug	27.4	44.3	61.5	70.8	76.6	80.4
Public order*	30.0	48.1	64.3	72.1	77.0	80.7
30–34	28.0%	43.4%	60.0%	68.1%	73.4%	77.0%
Violent	25.1	38.6	54.9	62.4	68.2	72.0
Property	33.8	50.9	68.3	76.0	80.7	83.7
Drug	25.5	41.2	58.4	66.8	72.2	76.1
Public order*	27.5	42.3	56.4	66.0	71.2	75.2
35–39	29.2%	44.4%	61.2%	69.8%	74.7%	78.1%
Violent	26.7	42.1	59.6	66.1	70.6	74.0
Property	35.0	52.8	69.3	77.6	81.9	83.8
Drug	27.8	40.7	56.7	67.0	72.8	77.0
Public order*	24.1	38.0	56.0	64.9	70.3	74.8
40 or older	24.0%	37.3%	52.1%	60.3%	65.5%	69.2%
Violent	20.3	31.5	43.4	50.3	56.0	60.7
Property	29.8	44.9	61.2	69.0	73.8	76.9
Drug	24.6	38.7	54.2	62.5	67.6	71.2
Public order*	17.6	28.8	44.4	55.3	60.6	63.9

Note: Prisoners were tracked for 5 years following release. Inmates could have been in prison for more than one offense; the most serious one is reported in this table. Data on prisoner's age were known for 100% of cases. See appendix table 15 for standard errors.

*Includes 0.8% of cases in which the prisoner's most serious offense was unspecified.

Source: Bureau of Justice Statistics, Recidivism of State Prisoners Released in 2005 data collection.

By the end of the fifth year after release, black inmates had the highest recidivism rate among all racial or ethnic groups

One year after release from prison, non-Hispanic black (45.8%) and Hispanic (46.3%) inmates had been arrested at similar rates. In comparison, non-Hispanic white inmates (39.7%) had lower recidivism rates within the first year of release than black and Hispanic inmates (figure 7 and table 15). Over the next 4 years, the recidivism rate for Hispanics did not increase as much as that for blacks. By the end of the fifth year after release from prison, white (73.1%) and Hispanic (75.3%) offenders had lower recidivism rates than black offenders (80.8%).

From at least 6 months after release from prison through the end of the 5-year follow-up period, black offenders had higher rates of recidivism than white offenders. This pattern generally held, regardless of the type of offense for which the inmate was imprisoned. Three years after release, 55.6% of white inmates who were imprisoned for a violent crime had been arrested for a new offense, compared to 66.4% of black inmates. By the end of the fifth year after release, these proportions for inmates who were imprisoned for a violent crime increased to 65.1% for white and 76.9% for black inmates.

FIGURE 7
Recidivism of prisoners released in 30 states in 2005, by race or Hispanic origin and time from release to first arrest

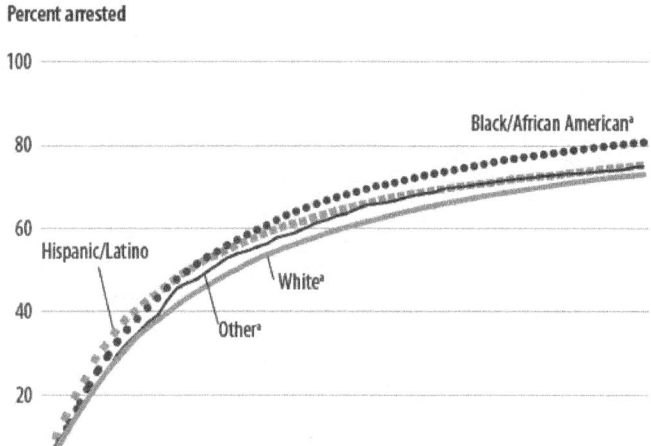

Note: Prisoners were tracked for 5 years following release. Data on prisoner's race or Hispanic origin were known for nearly 100% of cases.

[a]Excludes persons of Hispanic or Latino origin.

[b]Includes persons identified as American Indian or Alaska Native; Asian, Native Hawaiian, or other Pacific Islander; and persons of other races.

Source: Bureau of Justice Statistics, Recidivism of State Prisoners Released in 2005 data collection.

TABLE 15
Recidivism of prisoners released in 30 states in 2005, by race or Hispanic origin, most serious commitment offense, and time from release to first arrest

Race/Hispanic origin and most serious commitment offense	Cumulative percent of released prisoners arrested within—					
	6 months	1 year	2 years	3 years	4 years	5 years
All released prisoners	28.2%	43.4%	59.5%	67.8%	73.0%	76.6%
White[a]	25.6%	39.7%	55.5%	63.9%	69.3%	73.1%
Violent	21.9	33.6	48.2	55.6	61.1	65.1
Property	31.2	47.6	63.9	71.9	76.9	80.0
Drug	23.6	37.7	53.4	62.4	68.2	72.6
Public order[b]	21.5	33.9	50.1	60.2	65.6	69.5
Black/African American[a]	29.1%	45.8%	63.2%	71.7%	77.2%	80.8%
Violent	26.1	41.5	58.1	66.4	72.6	76.9
Property	33.9	51.3	68.5	76.5	81.8	84.5
Drug	28.5	45.5	63.7	72.6	77.9	81.5
Public order[b]	27.3	44.4	61.4	69.9	75.3	79.1
Hispanic/Latino	32.3%	46.3%	60.7%	68.1%	72.2%	75.3%
Violent	28.1	40.9	54.9	62.7	67.5	71.3
Property	39.8	55.7	71.1	77.6	80.2	83.0
Drug	29.0	42.2	57.0	65.0	69.8	72.5
Public order[b]	34.9	50.4	61.7	68.4	72.2	75.9
Other[a,c]	25.7%	42.7%	58.3%	67.3%	72.1%	75.0%
Violent	19.9	34.7	51.9	58.9	62.0	66.6
Property	36.5	55.4	69.3	78.3	81.6	83.7
Drug	19.4	39.5	57.0	67.3	76.5	78.1
Public order[b]	23.0	37.3	51.1	62.4	68.4	71.2

Note: Prisoners were tracked for 5 years following release. Inmates could have been in prison for more than one offense; the most serious one is reported in this table. Data on the prisoner's race or Hispanic origin were known for nearly 100% of cases. See appendix table 16 for standard errors.

[a]Excludes persons of Hispanic or Latino origin.

[b]Includes 0.8% of cases in which the prisoner's most serious offense was unspecified.

[c]Includes persons identified as American Indian or Alaska Native; Asian, Native Hawaiian, or other Pacific Islander; and persons of other races.

Source: Bureau of Justice Statistics, Recidivism of State Prisoners Released in 2005 data collection.

Recidivism rates across the 5-year follow-up period for black and Hispanic inmates differed by commitment offense. For example, the recidivism rates at the end of the first year for inmates committed for a violent or drug offense were similar for both groups. By the fifth year after release, the recidivism rates for Hispanics were lower than those for blacks committed for violent or drug crimes.

Other measures of recidivism

An arrest is one of many possible measures of recidivism. In this study, four additional measures (i.e., adjudication, conviction, incarceration, and imprisonment) were prepared using criminal history records. These measures were based on prisoners released from the 29 states in the study that had the necessary data. A fifth measure—return to prison—was prepared using a combination of criminal history records and the records of state departments of corrections. This measure was based on prisoners released from 23 of the 30 states.

Because the various measures of recidivism set different criteria for labeling a person as a recidivist, the percentage of inmates classified as recidivists declined as the recidivism measurement progressed from arrest to adjudication to conviction to incarceration to imprisonment. Any use of these recidivism rates must take into account the quality and completeness of the data found in rap sheets. (See *Methodology* for more information.)

Adjudication—Classifies persons as a recidivist when an arrest resulted in the matter being sent deeper into the criminal justice system to be sanctioned by a court. An estimated 49.8% of inmates had an arrest within 3 years of release that resulted in the matter being referred to criminal court for adjudication, and 60.0% had an arrest within 5 years of release that resulted in an adjudication (figure 8 and table 16).

Conviction—Classifies persons as a recidivist if the court has determined the individual committed a new crime. An estimated 45.2% of inmates had an arrest within 3 years of release that resulted in a conviction in criminal court, and 55.4% of inmates had an arrest within 5 years that resulted in a conviction.

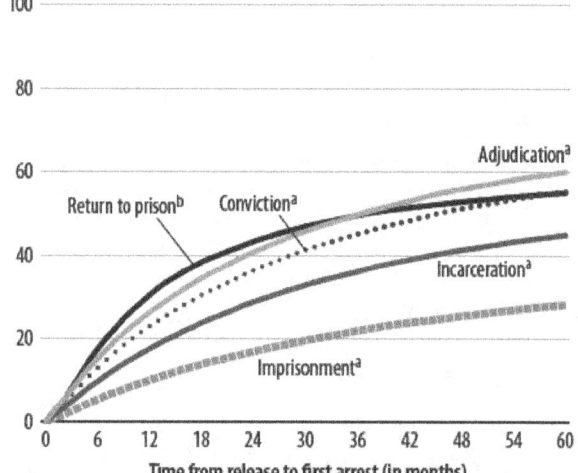

FIGURE 8

Recidivism of prisoners released in 29 states in 2005, by time from release to first arrest that led to recidivating event

Percent of who reddivated

Note: Prisoners were tracked for 5 years following release in 30 states. Some states were excluded from the specific measures of recidivism. See *Methodology*.

[a]Based on time from release to first arrest that led to recidivating event (i.e., adjudication, conviction, incarceration, or imprisonment) among inmates released in 29 states.

[b]Based on time from release to first arrest that led to a prison sentence or first prison admission for a technical violation without a new sentence among inmates released in 23 states.

Source: Bureau of Justice Statistics, Recidivism of State Prisoners Released in 2005 data collection.

Continued on next page.

Other measures of recidivism (continued)

Incarceration—Classifies persons as a recidivist when an arrest resulted in a prison or jail sentence. An estimated 36.2% of inmates had an arrest within 3 years of release that resulted in a conviction with a disposition of a jail or prison sentence, compared to 44.9% within 5 years of release.

Imprisonment—Classifies persons as a recidivist when an arrest resulted in a prison sentence. Among inmates who had an arrest that resulted in a conviction with a disposition of a prison sentence, 22.0% were within 3 years of release, and 28.2% were within 5 years of release.

Return to prison—Classifies persons as a recidivist when an arrest resulted in a conviction with a disposition of a prison sentence or when the offender was returned to prison without a new conviction because of a technical violation of his or her release, such as failing a drug test or missing an appointment with a parole officer. Within 3 years of release, 49.7% of inmates either had an arrest that resulted in a conviction with

a disposition of a prison sentence or were returned to prison without a new conviction because they violated a technical condition of their release, as did 55.1% of inmates within 5 years of release.

Returning to prison is probably the most common measure used in the field when studying the recidivism of released inmates. Among inmates in this study who returned to prison 1 year after release in 2005, property crime offenders (36.4%) had the highest percentage of recidivism. The 1-year return-to-prison percentages for violent (27.5%), drug (28.1%), and public order (27.7%) inmates were equal, and all were lower than that of property offenders. Five years after release from prison, the return-to-prison rate of inmates committed for a property offense (61.8%) remained higher than the return-to-prison rates of inmates committed for a violent (50.6%), drug (53.3%), or public order (52.6%) offense.

TABLE 16
Recidivism of prisoners released in 29 states in 2005, by most serious commitment offense and time from release to first arrest that led to recidivating event

Recidivism measurement and most serious commitment offense	Cumulative percent of released prisoners who recidivated within—					
	6 months	1 year	2 years	3 years	4 years	5 years
Adjudication[a]	15.2%	26.3%	40.7%	49.8%	55.9%	60.0%
Violent	11.7	20.6	33.7	41.7	48.0	52.6
Property	18.6	31.8	46.9	56.2	62.1	66.1
Drug	15.4	26.3	41.7	51.1	57.1	61.0
Public order[b]	14.0	24.7	38.6	48.4	54.6	58.5
Conviction[a]	13.0%	23.0%	36.3%	45.2%	51.3%	55.4%
Violent	9.8	17.6	29.5	37.2	43.4	48.0
Property	16.0	27.9	42.1	51.5	57.3	61.2
Drug	13.1	23.0	37.2	46.1	52.3	56.3
Public order[b]	12.0	22.2	34.8	44.7	50.5	54.2
Incarceration[a]	9.8%	17.5%	28.8%	36.2%	41.3%	44.9%
Violent	7.7	13.9	23.5	29.8	35.0	38.9
Property	12.1	21.5	33.5	41.6	46.9	50.6
Drug	9.4	17.0	29.0	36.1	41.2	44.6
Public order[b]	9.3	17.1	27.9	36.7	41.6	44.7
Imprisonment[a]	5.4%	10.0%	16.9%	22.0%	25.5%	28.2%
Violent	4.2	7.5	13.2	17.3	20.3	22.9
Property	7.2	13.0	20.7	26.5	30.3	33.4
Drug	4.8	9.4	16.4	21.5	25.1	27.6
Public order[b]	4.9	9.6	16.6	22.2	25.8	28.2
Return to prison[c]	17.6%	30.4%	43.3%	49.7%	52.9%	55.1%
Violent	16.2	27.5	39.5	45.4	48.4	50.6
Property	21.8	36.4	49.6	56.2	59.5	61.8
Drug	15.4	28.1	41.8	48.0	51.2	53.3
Public order[b]	16.1	27.7	39.4	46.7	50.1	52.6

Note: Prisoners were tracked for 5 years following release in 30 states. Some states were excluded from the specific measures of recidivism. See *Methodology*. Inmates could have been in prison for more than one offense; the most serious one is reported in this table. See appendix table 17 for standard errors.

[a]Based on time from release to first arrest that led to recidivating event (i.e., adjudication, conviction, incarceration, or imprisonment) among inmates released in 29 states.

[b]Includes 0.8% of cases in which the prisoner's most serious offense was unspecified.

[c]Based on time from release to first arrest that led to a prison sentence or first prison admission for a technical violation without a new sentence among inmates released in 23 states.

Source: Bureau of Justice Statistics, Recidivism of State Prisoners Released in 2005 data collection.

Methodology

Background

In 2008, the Bureau of Justice Statistics (BJS) entered into a data sharing agreement with the FBI's Criminal Justice Information Services (CJIS) Division and the International Justice and Public Safety Network (Nlets) to provide BJS access to criminal history records (i.e., rap sheets) through the FBI's Interstate Identification Index (III). A data security agreement was executed between BJS, the FBI, and Nlets to define the operational and technical practices used to protect the confidentiality and integrity of the criminal history data during exchange, processing, and storage.

The FBI's III is an automated pointer system that allows authorized agencies to determine whether any state repository has criminal history records on an individual. Nlets is a computer-based network that is responsible for the interstate transmissions of federal and state criminal history records. It allows users to query III and send requests to states holding criminal history records on an individual. The FBI also maintains criminal history records that they are solely responsible for disseminating. The identification bureaus that operate the central repositories in each state respond automatically to requests over the Nlets network. Responses received via Nlets represent an individual's national criminal history record.

Under the Criminal History Records Information Sharing (CHRIS) Project (award 2008-BJ-CX-K040), Nlets developed an automated collection system for BJS to retrieve national criminal history records from the FBI and state repositories on large samples of study subjects. Nlets produced software to parse the fields from individual criminal history records into a relational database. The database consists of state- and federal-specific numeric codes and text descriptions (e.g., criminal statutes and case outcome information) in a uniform record layout. In September 2010, BJS and Nlets conducted a pilot test of the data collection system and rap sheet parsing programs to ensure the software could handle the wide variations in the nation's criminal history records.

The Conversion of Criminal History Records into Research Databases (CCHRRD) Project (grant 2009-BJ-CX-K058) funded NORC at the University of Chicago to develop software that standardizes the content of the relational database produced by Nlets into a uniform coding structure that supports national-level recidivism research. The 2005 prisoner recidivism study was the first project to use the systems developed under the CHRIS and CCHRRD projects. The electronic records accessed by BJS through III for this study are the same records used by police officers to determine the current criminal justice status (e.g., on probation, parole, or bail) of a suspect; by judges to make pretrial and sentencing decisions; and by corrections officials to determine inmate classifications, parole releases, and work furloughs.

Sampling

States were selected for the study based on their ability to provide prisoner records and the FBI or state identification numbers on persons released from correctional facilities in 2005. The fingerprint-based identification numbers were needed to obtain criminal history records on the released prisoners. The prisoner records—obtained from the state departments of corrections through BJS's National Corrections Reporting Program (NCRP)—also included each inmate's date of birth, sex, race, Hispanic origin, confinement offenses, sentence length, type of prison admission and release, and date of release. The 30 states that supplied BJS with the required data included Alaska, Arkansas, California, Colorado, Florida, Georgia, Hawaii, Iowa, Louisiana, Maryland, Michigan, Minnesota, Missouri, Nebraska, Nevada, New Jersey, New York, North Carolina, North Dakota, Ohio, Oklahoma, Oregon, Pennsylvania, South Carolina, South Dakota, Texas, Utah, Virginia, Washington, and West Virginia. Among each of these states, the percentage of prisoner records with a state or FBI identification number ranged from 93% to 100%, and averaged 99% (not shown).

Of the 544,728 inmates released in the study's 30 states in 2005, 412,731 met BJS's selection criteria for this study (table 17). The study excluded releases that were transfers to the custody of another authority, releases due to death, releases on bond, releases to seek or participate in an appeal of a case, and escapes from prison or absent without official leave (AWOL). Inmates whose sentence was less than 1 year were also excluded. The first release during 2005 was selected for persons released multiple times during the year.

BJS drew a systematic random sample of eligible cases from each of the 30 states. Sex was used to stratify the sampling frame within each state. The eligible cases were then separated into 16 categories based on the most serious prison commitment offense. The sampling design included all individuals who were in prison for homicide. Before selecting the sample, prison records of persons committed for a nonhomicide offense were grouped by sex, and then sorted by the county in which the sentence was imposed, race, Hispanic origin, age, and commitment offense. The sampling rate for female prisoners was doubled to improve

the precision of their recidivism estimates. A total of 70,878 released prisoners were randomly selected to represent the 412,731 released in 2005 in the 30 states. Each prisoner in the sample was assigned a weight based on the probability of selection within the state.

Collecting and processing criminal records for recidivism research

BJS received approval from the FBI's Institutional Review Board to access criminal history records through III for this study. This study employed a 5-year follow-up period, two years longer than found in previous BJS recidivism studies. In June 2011, BJS sent the state and FBI identification numbers supplied by the departments of corrections to III via Nlets to collect the criminal history records on the 70,878 former prisoners. These criminal history records contain information from the state that released them, as well as all other states in the U.S., and records covering events prior to and following their release in 2005. Over a

TABLE 17
Number of prisoners released in 30 states in 2005

State	Number of released prisoners[a]	Number of sample cases	Released prisoners included in the study[b]		Criminal history record collected	
			Weighted total	Sample size	Number	Percent
All released prisoners	412,731	70,878	404,638	69,279	68,597	99.0%
Alaska	1,827	1,158	1,764	1,118	1,099	98.3
Arkansas	10,844	2,785	10,513	2,697	2,640	97.9
California	107,633	4,604	106,116	4,542	4,541	100
Colorado	8,277	2,351	8,042	2,281	2,275	99.7
Florida	31,537	3,350	30,975	3,285	3,272	99.6
Georgia	12,321	2,763	12,054	2,697	2,602	96.5
Hawaii	1,041	793	1,022	779	772	99.1
Iowa	4,607	1,897	4,465	1,839	1,836	99.8
Louisiana	12,876	2,806	12,552	2,737	2,723	99.5
Maryland	10,200	2,597	9,859	2,513	2,494	99.2
Michigan	12,177	2,603	11,775	2,519	2,504	99.4
Minnesota	4,619	1,897	4,581	1,882	1,879	99.8
Missouri	15,997	2,919	15,513	2,828	2,823	99.8
Nebraska	1,386	966	1,366	952	952	100
Nevada	5,022	1,973	4,965	1,949	1,808	92.8
New Jersey	13,097	2,697	12,992	2,674	2,630	98.4
New York	23,963	3,532	23,448	3,459	3,459	100
North Carolina	11,743	2,748	11,335	2,653	2,643	99.6
North Dakota	884	686	868	674	666	98.8
Ohio	15,832	3,070	15,688	3,038	2,966	97.6
Oklahoma	7,768	2,345	7,459	2,250	2,184	97.1
Oregon	4,731	1,955	4,625	1,912	1,910	99.9
Pennsylvania	12,452	2,840	12,020	2,741	2,714	99.0
South Carolina	10,046	2,537	9,982	2,519	2,512	99.7
South Dakota	2,159	1,285	2,151	1,280	1,275	99.6
Texas	43,532	3,779	43,118	3,742	3,742	100
Utah	3,000	1,569	2,974	1,556	1,548	99.5
Virginia	12,776	2,719	12,319	2,619	2,609	99.6
Washington	8,439	2,443	8,234	2,382	2,380	99.9
West Virginia	1,945	1,211	1,864	1,162	1,139	98.0

[a]Excludes releases of prisoners whose sentence was less than 1 year, releases to custody/detainer/warrant, releases due to death, escapes or being absent without leave, transfers, administrative releases, and releases on appeal. The first release was selected for persons released multiple times during 2005.

[b]Excludes 1,595 sampled prisoners who died during the 5-year follow-up period and four cases determined to be invalid release records.

Source: Bureau of Justice Statistics, Recidivism of State Prisoners Released in 2005 data collection.

3-week period, Nlets electronically collated the responses received from the FBI and state criminal history repositories into a relational database.

The criminal history information on the sampled prisoners from 30 states included over 800,000 pre- and post-release arrests and dispositions from more than 25,000 criminal justice agencies in all 50 states and the District of Columbia. BJS conducted a series of data quality checks on the criminal history records to assess the accuracy and completeness of the information, beginning with an examination of the response messages and the identification numbers that failed to match a record in III. In August 2011, BJS had Nlets submit a separate set of record requests directly to the state repositories for cases in which the original request in June did not produce criminal history information. These secondary requests provided additional criminal history records that were not available through III.

To ensure that the correct records were received on the released prisoners using their fingerprint-based identification numbers, BJS compared other individual identifiers in the NCRP data to those reported in the criminal history records. A released prisoner's date of birth in the NCRP data exactly matched his or her birthdate in the criminal history records 98% of the time. Nearly 100% of the NCRP and criminal history records matched on sex and race at the person level.

This report relied on a combination of arrest charge, court disposition, incarceration sentence, and custody information to measure recidivism. Juvenile offenses were rarely included in the criminal history records unless the offender was charged or tried in court as an adult. BJS reviewed the composition of information reported in the criminal history records for distributional differences and inconsistencies in reporting practices and observed some variations across states. During the data processing and analysis phases, steps were taken to standardize the information used to measure recidivism and to minimize the impact these variations had on the overall recidivism estimates.

For example, administrative (e.g., a criminal registration or the issuance of a warrant) and procedural (e.g., transferring a suspect to another jurisdiction) records embedded in the arrest data that did not refer to an actual arrest were identified and removed from the study. Traffic violations (with the exception of vehicular manslaughter, driving while intoxicated, and hit-and-run) were also excluded from the study because the coverage of these events in the criminal history records varied widely by state.

The criminal history records from some states recorded sentence modifications that occurred after the original court disposition and sentence while records from other states did not. To ensure consistent counting rules were employed when measuring recidivism across states, the initial court disposition was captured for an arrest charge when subsequent sentence modifications were also reported within the same arrest cycle. For instance, if a court adjudication was originally deferred and then later modified to a conviction, the deferred adjudication was coded as the disposition for that arrest charge.

To assess the completeness of the adjudication and incarceration information reported in the criminal history records, BJS attempted to identify an incarceration sentence (within the state where the release occurred) in each prisoner's criminal history prior to the date of his or her most recent prison admission before being released in 2005 according to the NCRP. Overall, 93% of the cases had a criminal history record that met these criteria.

Most criminal history records reported detailed information on the offender's adjudicated guilt or innocence and, if convicted, on the sentence imposed (e.g., prison, jail, or probation). BJS examined the disposition rates and found the proportion of arrests with a court disposition varied across states. This could be due to natural variations in state practices. However, the variations may be caused by either a lack of reporting court dispositions to the state repository or the inability of the repository to connect a reported court disposition to a specific arrest. BJS also found in some states that disposition information for certain arrests, such as arrests for failure to appear or contempt of court, was sometimes reported back on the earlier arrest for the underlying crime.

One aspect of recidivism measured in this study was a return to prison for a technical parole or other community supervision violation (e.g., failing a drug test or missing an appointment with a probation officer) or a sentence for a new crime. BJS found that the availability of the information on technical violations varied in the criminal history records by state likely because those types of returns to prison may not involve a new court sentence. Given the inconsistent reporting of such custody information in the criminal history records, the annual prison admission records from the NCRP were used to supplement the criminal history data to capture returns to prison with or without a sentence for a new crime. Analyzing the NCRP data, BJS used a set of individual identifiers (e.g., state identification number, inmate identification number, date of birth, sex, and race) to locate information on new prison admissions for a study subject during the 5 years following release in 2005. Using this information in combination with incarcerations recorded on the rap sheets, BJS identified released prisoners who returned to prison within the 5-year recidivism window.

Adjustment of sample weights

Deaths

BJS determined that 1,595 of the 70,878 sampled prisoners died during the 5-year follow-up period. Initial identification of sampled prisoners who died within the 5-year follow-up period was done using death information contained on the rap sheets. Additional deaths were identified by probabilistically linking sampled prisoners to individuals identified as dead in the Social Security Administration's (SSA) public Death Master File (DMF).

Specifically, linkplus, a probabilistic record linkage program developed by CDC, was used to create and score potential matches between the released prisoners' records and the public DMF, using common information found on each file (i.e., social security number (SSN), first name, last name, and date of birth (DOB))[1]. For persons with multiple SSNs, names and DOBs, all possible combinations (over 3.5 million unique permutations) were tested for matches. Based on the framework and decision rules as proposed by Fellegi and Sunter (1969), the software computed a probabilistic record linkage score for each matched record, with the score representing the sum of the agreement and disagreement weights for each matching variable; the higher the score, the greater the likelihood that the match made is a true match.[2] In order to differentiate true matches from false matches, the scores of the linked records were manually evaluated to ascertain the appropriate upper and lower bound cutoff scores. During this review, it was determined that records with a score of 20.0 or higher were exact matches of name, SSN, and DOB, and scores of less than 10.9 indicated none of the personally identifiable information matched. Accordingly, these cutoffs were used as the upper and lower cutoff scores to automatically designate true matches and nonmatches. All remaining pairs that fell between the upper and lower cutoff scores were manually reviewed by two independent reviewers and independently categorized and all discrepancies where the reviewers did not agree (less than 1%) were jointly classified.

Of importance, the number of released prisoners who were identified as dead in the DMF likely represents an undercount of the actual number of deaths within the sample. This is due, in part, to the limitations of the public DMF. Specifically, due to state disclosure laws, the public DMF does not include information on certain protected state death records (defined as records received via SSA's contracts with the states). This change, which occurred in November 2011, resulted in SSA removing over 4.2 million state-reported death records from the public DMF and

---

[1]Link Plus Version 2.10 probabilistic record linkage software. Atlanta, GA: Centers for Disease Control and Prevention, 2006.

[2]Fellegi, I. P., & Sunter, A. B. (1969). A theory for record linkage. *Journal of the American Statistical Association*, 64, 1183–12.

adding over 1 million fewer records annually to the current public DMF thereafter. As a result, the public DMF contains an undercount of annual deaths.

It is unknown precisely how extensively the public DMF undercounts the annual number of deaths. Preliminary analyses comparing the number of deaths in the public DMF to those reported via the Centers for Disease Control and Prevention's (CDC) mortality counts suggest that in 2005 the public DMF undercounted the overall number of deaths in the United States by around 10%. The undercount has increased each year since 2005. As of 2010 the public DMF contained around half (45%) of the deaths reported by the CDC (not shown). Furthermore, the coverage of the public DMF differs by decedent age, with younger decedents being less likely to appear in the public file. Because of this, it is likely that the death count of prisoners released in 2005 is an undercount of the actual number of deaths within the sample.

The 1,595 prisoners who died during the follow-up period were excluded from the study, along with four additional cases that were later determined to be invalid release records. When weighted, these 1,599 cases represented 8,092 prison releases. Therefore, the study's sample of 69,279 eligible prisoners is statistically representative of the 404,638 prisoners released in 2005 who were identified as living for at least 5 years after their dates of release.

Missing criminal history records

Among the 69,279 eligible prisoners sampled from 30 states, BJS did not obtain criminal history records on 406 subjects because the departments of corrections were unable to provide their FBI or state identification number. An additional 276 prisoners had an identification number, but no criminal history record linked to this number was found in the FBI or state record repositories. To account for the missing data, the original sample weights for the cases with complete criminal history information required adjustment. The sample weights for the 682 cases without a criminal history record were equally distributed among the weights of the 68,597 cases with the same commitment offense, demographic characteristics (i.e., sex, race, Hispanic origin, and age category), and state where released. The adjusted weights for the final sample of 68,597 persons were used to produce recidivism estimates on the 404,638 persons released from prison in the 30 states in 2005.

Conducting tests of statistical significance

Because this study was based on a sample and not a complete enumeration, the estimates in this report are subject to sampling error (i.e., a discrepancy between an estimate and a population parameter based on chance). One measure of the sampling error associated with an estimate is the standard error. The standard error can vary from one estimate to the next. In general, for a given metric, an estimate with a smaller standard error provides a more reliable approximation of the true value than an estimate with a larger standard error. Estimates with relatively large standard errors are associated with less precision and reliability and should be interpreted with caution. BJS conducted tests to determine whether differences in estimated numbers and percentages were statistically significant once sampling error was taken into account.

All differences discussed in this report are statistically significant at or above the 95% confidence interval. Standard errors were generated using SUDAAN, a statistical software package that estimates sampling error from complex sample surveys. Standard errors for each table are available at the end of the report.

Computing population-adjusted estimates of recidivism for the 1994 and 2005 studies

To examine how the recidivism rates from this study compared with those found in the previous one that measured the recidivism of prisoners released in 1994, BJS limited the comparison to the post-release arrest rates among inmates released from state prisons in the 12 states that were in both studies (California, Florida, Maryland, Michigan, Minnesota, New Jersey, New York, North Carolina, Ohio, Oregon, Texas, and Virginia). To control for the compositional differences in the types of prisoners released in these states during 1994 and 2005, RTI International (RTI) assisted BJS with standardizing the distribution of the 2005 prison release cohort to the distribution of the 1994 prison release cohort based on the following categorical variables.

- Sex (male or female)

- Age at release (24 or younger, 25 to 29, 30 to 34, 35 to 39, or 40 or older)

- Race/Hispanic origin (non-Hispanic white, non-Hispanic black, Hispanic, or other race)

- Most serious prison commitment offense (violent, property, drug, or public order).

RTI used SUDAAN software to generate the standardized estimates and determine whether any differences between the estimates for 1994 and 2005 cohorts were statistically significant. The following procedures were used to complete the analysis.

1. Missing data on the demographic characteristics and commitment offenses of the inmates were imputed using a stochastic imputation approach, which determined the cumulative distribution function (CDF) for the characteristic being imputed based on inmates with a known value for the characteristic. Inmates with a missing value were randomly assigned a value based on the CDF. For age at release, the CDF was conditioned on the sex of the inmate. For all other characteristics, the CDF was conditioned on the sex and age at release

of the inmate. Data on the sex of inmates released in 1994 were known for 100% of cases, race and Hispanic origin for 99.9%, age at release for nearly 100%, and commitment offense for 99.9%. Data on sex of inmates released in 2005 were known for 100% of cases, race and Hispanic origin for 99.8%, age at release for 100%, and commitment offense for 99.8%.

2. A joint probability distribution was produced of inmates in the 1994 cohort based on sex, age at release, race/Hispanic origin, and most serious commitment offense. This distribution documented the proportion of the 1994 cohort that fell into each of 160 specific inmate subpopulations defined by crossing five categories of age, two categories of sex, four categories of race/Hispanic origin, and four categories of commitment offenses.

3. In order to allow for simultaneous estimation and comparisons, a stacked file was created containing the records on both the 1994 cohort and the 2005 cohort. A new variable (called GROUP) was created to distinguish in which cohort the inmate resided (1=1994 and 2=2005).

4. The PROC DESCRIPT procedure in SUDAAN was used to generate the standardized point estimates. This approach standardized the estimates for the 2005 cohort to the probability distribution of the 1994 cohort obtained in step 2.

   a. The standard errors for the standardized estimates were calculated in SUDAAN with a "without replacement" sample design (DESIGN = WOR).

   b. The sampling weights for the 1994 and 2005 studies were assigned in the WEIGHT statement.

   c. A single variable that accounted for the unique sample designs of the 1994 and 2005 studies was specified in the NEST statement.

   d. In the STDVAR statement, the four imputed inmate characteristic variables were listed in the order the probability distribution was created— sex, age, race/Hispanic origin, and commitment offense. These variables were also listed in the CLASS statement.

   e. The joint probability distribution of the 1994 cohort was listed in the STDWGT statement.

   f. In the TABLE statement, the GROUP variable was crossed with each of the nonimputed inmate characteristics. In other words, an index combining the cohort identifier and each of the inmate characteristics was specified. This generated a separate marginal recidivism estimate for each set of inmate characteristics by cohort year.

g. The recidivism outcome variables of interest (i.e., arrested for any type of crime and arrested for a violent crime) were listed in the VAR statement.

h. The mean (MEAN) and standard error of the mean (SEMEAN) were calculated, imported into a table, and then converted into percentages by multiplying the proportions by 100.

5. The PROC DESCRIPT procedure was used to test the statistical differences for each inmate characteristic between the 1994 cohort and the standardized 2005 cohort. Using the PROC DESCRIPT procedure to conduct the test of differences allowed any correlation between the two cohort groups to be accounted for in the standard error of the test statistic.

a. The same DESIGN, WEIGHT, NEST, STDVAR, and STDWGT statements specified in step 4 were used to conduct the statistical significance tests.

b. The inmate characteristics were listed in the TABLE statement.

c. The same VAR statement was used from step 4.

d. The two levels in the GROUP variable were compared using the DIFFVAR statement.

e. In the CATLEVEL statement, the numeric code "1" was indicated to get the percentages of inmates who had a post-release arrest within 3 years.

f. The difference in the percentages (PERCENT), the standard error of the percentages (SEPERCENT), the test for the statistical difference (T_PCT), and the p-value for the test statistic (P_PCT) were imported into a table.

6. The p-value was used to determine which comparisons were significant at the 95% confidence interval, and those comparisons were assigned a symbol of "**."

Recidivism measures

This study measured six types of events to describe the recidivism of persons released from prison in 2005:

- **Arrest:** An arrest within 5 years of exiting prison in 2005. Information presented on the number of arrests is based on unique arrest dates, not individual charges.

- **Adjudication:** An arrest within 5 years of exiting prison in 2005 that resulted in a subsequent court adjudication or disposition (e.g., convictions, dismissals, acquittals, or deferred adjudications). Information on the number of adjudications is based on each unique arrest date that led to an adjudication, not the date of adjudication.

- **Conviction:** An arrest within 5 years of exiting prison in 2005 that resulted in a subsequent court conviction. Information on the number of convictions is based on each unique arrest date that led to a conviction, not the date of conviction.

- **Incarceration:** An arrest within 5 years of exiting prison in 2005 that resulted in a prison or jail sentence. Information on the number of incarcerations is based on each unique arrest date that led to a prison or jail sentence, not the date that the sentence was imposed.

- **Imprisonment:** An arrest within 5 years of exiting prison in 2005 that resulted in a prison sentence. When the type of facility (e.g., prison or jail) where an incarceration sentence was to be served was not reported in the criminal history records, a sentence of a year or more was defined as imprisonment. Information on the number of prison sentences is based on each unique arrest date that led to a prison sentence, not the date that the sentence was imposed.

The arrests that occurred within the 5-year follow-up period were tracked for an additional 6 months to determine whether the case outcomes led to an adjudication, conviction, incarceration, or imprisonment. These four measures were based on prisoners released in 29 of the study's 30 states. Louisiana prisoners were excluded because the disposition and sentencing information from that state was generally not linked to the associated arrest.

- **Return to prison:** An arrest or a technical violation of a condition of release within 5 years of exiting prison in 2005 that resulted in a return to prison. This recidivism measure incorporates the criminal history records from the FBI and state repositories and the prisoner records obtained from the state departments of corrections through the NCRP. The criminal history records provided information on arrests that resulted in incarceration during the 5-year follow-up period. BJS used the NCRP files from 2005 through 2010 to supplement the criminal history records with information on the released prisoners who returned to prison for a technical violation that did not involve a sentence for a new crime.

Prisoners released from Maryland, Nebraska, Nevada, Ohio, Pennsylvania, and Virginia were excluded from the return-to-prison analysis because the individual identifiers or complete prison admission data needed to locate returns to prison during the entire 2005 through 2010 observation window were not available. Louisiana prisoners were also excluded from the return-to-prison analysis because the sentencing information in the criminal history records from this state was generally not linked to the associated arrest.

Offense definitions

Violent offenses include homicide, rape or sexual assault, robbery, assault, and other miscellaneous or unspecified violent offenses.

Homicide includes murder, nonnegligent manslaughter, negligent manslaughter, and unspecified homicide offenses.

Murder is (1) intentionally causing the death of another person without extreme provocation or legal justification, or (2) causing the death of another while committing or attempting to commit another crime.

Nonnegligent (or voluntary) manslaughter is intentionally and without legal justification causing the death of another when acting under extreme provocation.

Negligent (or involuntary) manslaughter is causing the death of another person through recklessness or gross negligence, without intending to cause death. Negligent manslaughter also includes vehicular manslaughter, but excludes vehicular murder (intentionally killing someone with a motor vehicle), which is classified as murder.

Rape or sexual assault includes (1) forcible intercourse (vaginal, anal, or oral) with a female or male, (2) forcible sodomy or penetration with a foreign object (sometimes called "deviate sexual assault"), (3) forcible or violent sexual acts not involving intercourse with an adult or minor, (4) nonforcible sexual acts with a minor (such as statutory rape or incest with a minor), and (5) nonforcible sexual acts with someone unable to give legal or factual consent because of mental or physical defect or intoxication.

Robbery is the unlawful taking of property that is in the immediate possession of another, by force or the threat of force. Includes forcible purse snatching, but excludes nonforcible purse snatching.

Assault includes aggravated, simple and unspecified assault. Aggravated assault includes (1) intentionally and without legal justification causing serious bodily injury, with or without a deadly weapon, or (2) using a deadly or dangerous weapon to threaten, attempt, or cause bodily injury, regardless of the degree of injury, if any. The category also includes attempted murder, aggravated battery, felonious assault, and assault with a deadly weapon. Simple assault includes intentionally and without legal justification causing less than serious bodily injury without a deadly or dangerous weapon, or attempting or threatening bodily injury without a dangerous or deadly weapon.

Other violent offenses contain a range of crimes, including intimidation, illegal abortion, extortion, cruelty towards a child or wife, kidnapping, hit-and-run with bodily injury, and miscellaneous or unspecified crimes against the person.

Property offenses include burglary, fraud/forgery, larceny, motor vehicle theft, and other miscellaneous or unspecified property offenses.

Burglary is the unlawful entry of a fixed structure used for regular residence, industry, or business, with or without the use of force, to commit a felony or theft.

Larceny is the unlawful taking of property other than a motor vehicle from the possession of another, by stealth, without force or deceit. Includes pocket picking, nonforcible purse snatching, shoplifting, and thefts from motor vehicles. Excludes receiving or reselling stolen property or both, and thefts through fraud or deceit.

Motor vehicle theft is the unlawful taking of a self-propelled road vehicle owned by another. Includes the theft of automobiles, trucks, and motorcycles, but not the theft of boats, aircraft, or farm equipment (classified as larceny). Also includes receiving, possessing, stripping, transporting, and reselling stolen vehicles, and unauthorized use of a vehicle (joyriding).

Fraud/forgery includes using deceit or intentional misrepresentation to unlawfully deprive persons of his or her property or legal rights. It also includes offenses such as embezzlement, check fraud, confidence game, counterfeiting, and credit card fraud.

Other property offenses include arson, stolen property offenses, possession of burglary tools, damage to property, trespassing, and miscellaneous or unspecified property crimes.

Drug offenses include possession, trafficking, and other miscellaneous or unspecified drug offenses.

Drug possession includes possession of an illegal drug, but excludes possession with intent to sell. It also includes offenses involving drug paraphernalia and forged or unauthorized prescriptions.

Drug trafficking includes manufacturing, distributing, selling, smuggling, and possession with intent to sell.

Other drug offenses include offenses involving drug paraphernalia, forged or unauthorized prescriptions, and other miscellaneous or unspecified drug offenses.

Public order offenses include weapons offenses, driving under the influence, and other miscellaneous or unspecified offenses.

> **Weapons offenses** include the unlawful sale, distribution, manufacture, alteration, transportation, possession, or use of a deadly or dangerous weapon or accessory.

> **Driving under the influence (DUI)** is driving under the influence of drugs or alcohol and driving while intoxicated.

> **Other public order offenses** are those that violate the peace or order of the community or threaten the public health or safety through unacceptable conduct, interference with governmental authority, or the violation of civil rights or liberties. The category also includes probation or parole violation, escape, obstruction of justice, court offenses, nonviolent sex offenses, commercialized vice, family offenses, liquor law violations, bribery, invasion of privacy, disorderly conduct, contributing to the delinquency of a minor, and other miscellaneous or unspecified offenses.

APPENDIX TABLE 1
Standard errors for table 1: Characteristics of prisoners released in 12 states in 1994 and 2005

Characteristic	1994	2005
Sex		
Male	0.28%	--
Female	0.28	--
Race/Hispanic origin		
White	0.41%	0.38%
Black/African American	0.45	0.37
Hispanic/Latino	0.40	0.37
Other	0.08	0.13
Age at release		
24 or younger	0.37%	0.30%
25–29	0.40	0.32
30–34	0.40	0.30
35–39	0.35	0.30
40 or older	0.35	0.38
Most serious commitment offense		
Violent	0.11%	0.36%
Property	0.12	0.37
Drug	0.21	0.38
Public order	0.19	0.25

-- Less than 0.005%.

Source: Bureau of Justice Statistics, Recidivism of State Prisoners Released in 1994 and 2005 data collections.

APPENDIX TABLE 2
Standard errors for table 2: Population-adjusted percent of prisoners arrested for a new crime within 3 years following release in 12 states in 1994 and 2005, by demographic characteristics and most serious commitment offense

Characteristic	1994	2005
All released prisoners	0.41%	0.35%
Sex		
Male	0.43%	0.38%
Female	1.54	0.78
Race/Hispanic origin		
White	0.72%	0.60%
Black/African American	0.56	0.49
Hispanic/Latino	1.05	0.92
Other	4.66	2.70
Age at release		
24 or younger	0.81%	0.73%
25–29	0.87	0.75
30–34	0.89	0.89
35–39	1.01	0.86
40 or older	1.08	0.66
Most serious commitment offense		
Violent	0.69%	0.68%
Property	0.70	0.65
Drug	0.78	0.63
Public order	1.40	1.00

Source: Bureau of Justice Statistics, Recidivism of State Prisoners Released in 1994 and 2005 data collections.

APPENDIX TABLE 3
Standard errors for table 3: First arrest charge of prisoners arrested for a new crime within 3 years following release in 11 states in 1994 and 2005

Most serious arrest charge	1994	2005
Violent	0.47%	0.35%
Property	0.55	0.43
Drug	0.57	0.45
Public order	0.47	0.51
Estimated number of prisoners with a post-release arrest	1,053.17	978.74

Source: Bureau of Justice Statistics, Recidivism of State Prisoners Released in 1994 and 2005 data collections.

APPENDIX TABLE 4
Standard errors for table 4: Population-adjusted percent of prisoners arrested for a violent crime within 3 years following release in 11 states in 1994 and 2005, by demographic characteristics and most serious commitment offense

Characteristic	1994	2005
All released prisoners	0.39%	0.38%
Sex		
Male	0.41%	0.40%
Female	0.96	0.93
Race/Hispanic origin		
White	0.58%	0.58%
Black/African American	0.63	0.58
Hispanic/Latino	0.87	0.86
Other	3.07	5.17
Age at release		
24 or younger	0.93%	0.91%
25–29	0.85	0.86
30–34	0.84	0.85
35–39	0.85	0.85
40 or older	0.81	0.64
Most serious commitment offense		
Violent	0.73%	0.72%
Property	0.67	0.72
Drug	0.71	0.67
Public order	1.20	0.94

Source: Bureau of Justice Statistics, Recidivism of State Prisoners Released in 1994 and 2005 data collections.

APPENDIX TABLE 5
Standard errors for table 5: Characteristics of prisoners released in 30 states in 2005

Characteristic	Percent
Sex	
Male	--
Female	--
Race/Hispanic origin	
White	0.28%
Black/African American	0.27
Hispanic/Latino	0.26
Other	0.09
Age at release	
24 or younger	0.22%
25–29	0.24
30–34	0.22
35–39	0.22
40 or older	0.28
Most serious commitment offense	
Violent	0.26%
Property	0.28
Drug	0.28
Public order	0.18
Number of prior arrests per released prisoner	
2 or fewer	0.15%
3–4	0.18
5–9	0.27
10 or more	0.29
Mean number	0.06
Median number	0.05
Number of prior convictions per released prisoner	
Mean number	0.03
Median number	0.03

-- Less than 0.005%.

Source: Bureau of Justice Statistics, Recidivism of State Prisoners Released in 2005 data collection.

APPENDIX TABLE 6
Standard errors for table 6: Out-of-state arrests of prisoners released in 30 states in 2005 arrests

Out-of-state arrests	Percent
Prior to release	
1 or more	0.24%
1–4	0.21
5–9	0.11
10 or more	0.09
Post-release	
1 or more	0.16%
1–4	0.15
5–9	0.05
10 or more	0.02

Source: Bureau of Justice Statistics, Recidivism of State Prisoners Released in 2005 data collection.

APPENDIX TABLE 7
Standard errors for figure 2: Percent of prisoners arrested during the year who had not been arrested since release in 30 states in 2005

Year after release	Annual failure rate
Year 1	0.29%
Year 2	0.33
Year 3	0.34
Year 4	0.34
Year 5	0.34

Source: Bureau of Justice Statistics, Recidivism of State Prisoners Released in 2005 data collection.

APPENDIX TABLE 8
Standard errors for table 7: Post-release arrests of prisoners released in 30 states in 2005

Post-release arrests	Percent
None	0.23%
1	0.22
2	0.21
3	0.19
4	0.17
5	0.16
6 or more	0.24
Estimated number of post-release arrests	8,328.32
Mean number per released prisoners	0.02
Median number per released prisoners	0.02

Source: Bureau of Justice Statistics, Recidivism of State Prisoners Released in 2005 data collection.

Standard errors for table 8: Recidivism of prisoners released in 30 states in 2005, by most serious commitment offense and time from release to first arrest

Most serious commitment offense	Cumulative percent of released prisoners arrested within—					
	6 months	1 year	2 years	3 years	4 years	5 years
All released prisoners	0.28%	0.29%	0.27%	0.25%	0.24%	0.23%
Violent	0.56%	0.60%	0.58%	0.55%	0.52%	0.50%
Homicide	0.04	0.05	0.06	0.06	0.06	0.06
Murder	0.05	0.06	0.08	0.08	0.08	0.08
Nonnegligent manslaughter	0.12	0.16	0.18	0.19	0.19	0.19
Negligent manslaughter	0.06	0.08	0.09	0.10	0.10	0.10
Rape/sexual assault	1.19	1.33	1.37	1.35	1.33	1.30
Robbery	1.02	1.07	1.02	0.96	0.92	0.85
Assault	1.04	1.09	1.03	0.96	0.90	0.84
Other	2.25	2.27	2.12	2.01	1.94	1.85
Property	0.56%	0.55%	0.49%	0.45%	0.41%	0.39%
Burglary	0.87	0.88	0.80	0.73	0.68	0.64
Larceny/motor vehicle theft	1.06	1.01	0.89	0.81	0.75	0.71
Fraud/forgery	1.13	1.15	1.07	0.98	0.93	0.87
Other	1.63	1.62	1.44	1.26	1.13	1.06
Drug	0.51%	0.53%	0.50%	0.46%	0.43%	0.41%
Possession	1.00	1.04	0.97	0.90	0.82	0.78
Trafficking	0.78	0.82	0.77	0.72	0.68	0.65
Other	0.93	0.97	0.88	0.80	0.74	0.68
Public order	0.74%	0.77%	0.74%	0.70%	0.67%	0.64%
Weapons	1.92	1.87	1.66	1.51	1.43	1.36
Driving under the influence	1.07	1.24	1.38	1.41	1.39	1.36
Other	0.92	0.98	0.93	0.87	0.82	0.76

Source: Bureau of Justice Statistics, Recidivism of State Prisoners Released in 2005 data collection.

Standard errors for table 9: Recidivism of prisoners released in 30 states in 2005, by type of post-release arrest charge

Post-release arrest charge	Percent of released prisoners arrested within 5 years of release
Any offense	0.23%
Violent	0.27%
Homicide	0.06
Rape/sexual assault	0.08
Robbery	0.15
Assault	0.25
Other	0.12
Property	0.29%
Burglary	0.19
Larceny/motor vehicle theft	0.24
Fraud/forgery	0.20
Other	0.24
Drug	0.29%
Possession	0.27
Trafficking	0.21
Other	0.25
Public order	0.27%
Weapons	0.19
Driving under the influence	0.18
Probation/parole violation	0.26
Other	0.29

Source: Bureau of Justice Statistics, Recidivism of State Prisoners Released in 2005 data collection.

APPENDIX TABLE 11
Standard errors for table 10: Recidivism of prisoners released in 30 states in 2005, by type of post-release arrest charge and most serious commitment offense

Most serious commitment offense	Percent of released prisoners arrested within 5 years for —				
	Any offense	Violent offense	Property offense	Drug offense	Public order offense
All released prisoners	0.23%	0.27%	0.29%	0.29%	0.27%
Violent	0.50	0.57	0.55	0.56	0.57
Property	0.39	0.50	0.56	0.56	0.51
Drug	0.41	0.47	0.51	0.53	0.50
Public order	0.64	0.71	0.73	0.73	0.72

Source: Bureau of Justice Statistics, Recidivism of State Prisoners Released in 2005 data collection.

APPENDIX TABLE 12
Standard errors for table 11: Recidivism of prisoners released in 30 states in 2005, by prior arrest history, most serious commitment offense, and time from release to first arrest

Prior arrest history and most serious commitment offense	Cumulative percent of released prisoners arrested within—					
	6 months	1 year	2 years	3 years	4 years	5 years
All released prisoners	0.28%	0.29%	0.27%	0.25%	0.24%	0.23%
4 or fewer	0.38%	0.45%	0.48%	0.48%	0.47%	0.46%
Violent	0.60	0.72	0.78	0.80	0.80	0.79
Property	0.83	0.98	1.05	1.03	1.00	0.98
Drug	0.72	0.82	0.90	0.90	0.88	0.86
Public order	1.17	1.30	1.33	1.30	1.27	1.24
5–9	0.48%	0.52%	0.50%	0.47%	0.44%	0.42%
Violent	1.02	1.09	1.07	1.01	0.96	0.93
Property	0.95	0.98	0.91	0.83	0.77	0.72
Drug	0.76	0.86	0.84	0.79	0.73	0.70
Public order	1.24	1.32	1.31	1.27	1.22	1.16
10 or more	0.50%	0.48%	0.42%	0.38%	0.35%	0.32%
Violent	1.21	1.17	1.00	0.93	0.87	0.75
Property	0.85	0.80	0.66	0.59	0.53	0.50
Drug	0.90	0.87	0.77	0.69	0.63	0.58
Public order	1.27	1.28	1.14	1.02	0.96	0.92

Source: Bureau of Justice Statistics, Recidivism of State Prisoners Released in 2005 data collection.

APPENDIX TABLE 13

Standard errors for table 12: Recidivism of prisoners released in 30 states in 2005, by sex of releasee, most serious commitment offense, and time from release to first arrest

Sex of releasee and most serious commitment offense	Cumulative percent of released prisoners arrested within—					
	6 months	1 year	2 years	3 years	4 years	5 years
All released prisoners	0.28%	0.29%	0.27%	0.25%	0.24%	0.23%
Male	0.31%	0.32%	0.30%	0.28%	0.26%	0.25%
Violent	0.59	0.63	0.61	0.58	0.55	0.52
Property	0.63	0.62	0.55	0.50	0.46	0.44
Drug	0.57	0.59	0.55	0.51	0.48	0.45
Public order	0.80	0.83	0.80	0.75	0.71	0.68
Female	0.45%	0.49%	0.49%	0.48%	0.46%	0.44%
Violent	1.13	1.25	1.28	1.24	1.21	1.17
Property	0.79	0.85	0.84	0.80	0.76	0.73
Drug	0.77	0.83	0.83	0.80	0.78	0.75
Public order	1.20	1.36	1.42	1.39	1.34	1.30

Source: Bureau of Justice Statistics, Recidivism of State Prisoners Released in 2005 data collection.

APPENDIX TABLE 14

Standard errors for table 13: Post-release arrests of prisoners released in 30 states in 2005, by sex of releasee

Post-release arrests	Male	Female
None	0.25%	0.44%
1	0.25	0.38
2	0.23	0.36
3	0.21	0.31
4	0.19	0.28
5	0.17	0.27
6 or more	0.26	0.38
Estimated post-release arrests	8,193.63	1,491.77
Mean number	0.02	0.03
Median number	0.02	0.03

Source: Bureau of Justice Statistics, Recidivism of State Prisoners Released in 2005 data collection.

Standard errors for table 14: Recidivism of prisoners released in 30 states in 2005, by age at release, most serious commitment offense, and time from release to first arrest

Age at release and most serious commitment offense	Cumulative percent of released prisoners arrested within—					
	6 months	1 year	2 years	3 years	4 years	5 years
All released prisoners	0.28%	0.29%	0.27%	0.25%	0.24%	0.23%
24 or younger	0.69%	0.68%	0.60%	0.54%	0.49%	0.45%
Violent	1.34	1.38	1.27	1.17	1.10	0.99
Property	1.23	1.17	1.00	0.89	0.80	0.74
Drug	1.21	1.23	1.05	0.93	0.82	0.77
Public order	2.15	2.04	1.80	1.65	1.48	1.27
25–29	0.67%	0.68%	0.62%	0.55%	0.51%	0.48%
Violent	1.31	1.37	1.29	1.16	1.07	0.99
Property	1.33	1.31	1.15	1.02	0.94	0.88
Drug	1.11	1.15	1.05	0.94	0.86	0.82
Public order	1.88	1.89	1.70	1.55	1.43	1.35
30–34	0.73%	0.76%	0.71%	0.66%	0.63%	0.60%
Violent	1.45	1.53	1.48	1.41	1.34	1.29
Property	1.44	1.42	1.27	1.15	1.05	1.00
Drug	1.23	1.31	1.24	1.17	1.10	1.05
Public order	1.95	1.97	1.86	1.74	1.68	1.58
35–39	0.75%	0.77%	0.71%	0.65%	0.61%	0.57%
Violent	1.53	1.61	1.44	1.35	1.28	1.24
Property	1.40	1.37	1.21	1.05	0.96	0.92
Drug	1.35	1.38	1.32	1.22	1.14	1.06
Public order	1.73	1.84	1.82	1.75	1.68	1.59
40 or older	0.51%	0.54%	0.52%	0.50%	0.48%	0.46%
Violent	0.95	1.05	1.06	1.05	1.02	0.99
Property	1.02	1.04	0.96	0.90	0.85	0.81
Drug	0.95	1.01	0.95	0.89	0.85	0.81
Public order	1.09	1.18	1.26	1.22	1.18	1.16

Source: Bureau of Justice Statistics, Recidivism of State Prisoners Released in 2005 data collection.

Standard errors for table 15: Recidivism of prisoners released in 30 states in 2005, by race or Hispanic origin, most serious commitment offense, and time from release to first arrest

Race/Hispanic origin and most serious commitment offense	Cumulative percent of released prisoners arrested within—					
	6 months	1 year	2 years	3 years	4 years	5 years
All released prisoners	0.28%	0.29%	0.27%	0.25%	0.24%	0.23%
White	0.42%	0.44%	0.42%	0.39%	0.37%	0.35%
Violent	0.85	0.93	0.92	0.89	0.86	0.83
Property	0.75	0.74	0.67	0.61	0.57	0.54
Drug	0.88	0.93	0.87	0.81	0.75	0.71
Public order	0.90	0.97	0.98	0.93	0.89	0.86
Black/African American	0.41%	0.42%	0.39%	0.35%	0.33%	0.30%
Violent	0.80	0.83	0.77	0.71	0.66	0.59
Property	0.89	0.88	0.78	0.71	0.63	0.60
Drug	0.67	0.69	0.63	0.57	0.53	0.49
Public order	1.20	1.24	1.16	1.09	1.02	0.94
Hispanic/Latino	0.91%	0.93%	0.87%	0.81%	0.78%	0.75%
Violent	1.69	1.78	1.73	1.64	1.58	1.51
Property	1.88	1.84	1.60	1.46	1.41	1.32
Drug	1.50	1.57	1.50	1.40	1.33	1.30
Public order	2.68	2.68	2.53	2.38	2.29	2.19
Other	1.77%	1.97%	1.85%	1.71%	1.62%	1.57%
Violent	2.76	3.41	3.50	3.37	3.33	3.21
Property	3.79	3.58	3.17	2.56	2.47	2.43
Drug	2.98	4.57	4.47	4.18	3.40	3.37
Public order	3.15	3.45	3.43	3.30	3.27	3.27

Source: Bureau of Justice Statistics, Recidivism of State Prisoners Released in 2005 data collection.

Standard errors for table 16: Recidivism of prisoners released in 29 states in 2005, by most serious commitment offense and time from release to first arrest that led to recidivating event

Recidivism measurement and most serious commitment offense	Cumulative percent of released prisoners who recidivated within—					
	6 months	1 year	2 years	3 years	4 years	5 years
Adjudication	0.23%	0.27%	0.30%	0.31%	0.30%	0.30%
Violent	0.40	0.49	0.57	0.59	0.60	0.60
Property	0.46	0.54	0.57	0.57	0.56	0.55
Drug	0.42	0.50	0.54	0.55	0.54	0.53
Public order	0.58	0.68	0.76	0.78	0.78	0.77
Conviction	0.21%	0.26%	0.29%	0.30%	0.31%	0.30%
Violent	0.37	0.46	0.55	0.58	0.60	0.60
Property	0.43	0.52	0.56	0.57	0.57	0.56
Drug	0.39	0.47	0.53	0.55	0.55	0.54
Public order	0.55	0.67	0.75	0.78	0.78	0.78
Incarceration	0.19%	0.24%	0.28%	0.29%	0.30%	0.30%
Violent	0.35	0.43	0.51	0.55	0.58	0.59
Property	0.39	0.48	0.54	0.56	0.57	0.57
Drug	0.33	0.42	0.50	0.52	0.54	0.54
Public order	0.49	0.61	0.71	0.76	0.78	0.78
Imprisonment	0.15%	0.20%	0.24%	0.26%	0.27%	0.28%
Violent	0.27	0.34	0.43	0.47	0.50	0.53
Property	0.33	0.42	0.48	0.52	0.54	0.55
Drug	0.25	0.33	0.42	0.46	0.48	0.50
Public order	0.38	0.49	0.62	0.68	0.71	0.73
Return to prison	0.30%	0.33%	0.34%	0.33%	0.33%	0.33%
Violent	0.62	0.70	0.71	0.71	0.70	0.69
Property	0.61	0.65	0.64	0.62	0.61	0.60
Drug	0.52	0.60	0.62	0.62	0.61	0.61
Public order	0.80	0.91	0.93	0.91	0.90	0.89

Source: Bureau of Justice Statistics, Recidivism of State Prisoners Released in 2005 data collection.

www.ingramcontent.com/pod-product-compliance
Lightning Source LLC
Chambersburg PA
CBHW080754290526
45790CB00008B/3441